# A REVIEW OF THE IMPLEMENTATION OF THE CHILD SEXUAL ABUSE LEGISLATION IN SELECTED SITES

Joseph P. Hornick, Ph.D., Executive Director
Canadian Research Institute for Law and the Family

and

Floyd Bolitho, Ph.D.
Faculty of Social Work, The University of Calgary

1992

## CANADIAN CATALOGUING IN PUBLICATION DATA

Hornick, Joseph P. (Joseph Phillip), 1946-

A review of the implementation of the child sexual abuse legislation in selected sites

"The purpose of this report is to summarize and compare the findings of the site studies in Alberta, Saskatchewan, and Ontario." -- Executive summary.
Includes bibliographical references.

1. Sexually abused children -- Legal status, laws, etc. -- Canada. 2. Child molesting -- Law and legislation -- Canada. 3. Child abuse -- Law and legislation -- Canada. I. Bolitho, Floyd. II. Canada. Department of Justice. III. Title.

KE8926.H67 1992        345.71'02536        C93-099408-6

Published by authority of the Minister of Justice
and Attorney General of Canada
Government of Canada

by

Communications and Consultation Branch
Department of Justice Canada
Ottawa, Ontario
K1A 0H8

(613) 957-4222

ISBN 0-662-20238-4
DSS cat. no. JS42-51/2-1992E

JUS-P-637E

Également disponible en français sous le titre
Étude sur la mise en oeuvre des dispositions relatives à l'exploitaiton sexuelle d'enfants dans certaines localités

©Minister of Supply and Services Canada 1992

Printed in Canada

# TABLE OF CONTENTS

LIST OF FIGURES .................................................. viii

LIST OF TABLES ................................................... ix

ACKNOWLEDGMENTS ............................................. xi

EXECUTIVE SUMMARY ............................................ xiii

1.0 INTRODUCTION: LEGISLATIVE RESPONSE TO CHILD SEXUAL
    ABUSE ....................................................... 1

    1.1    Purpose of this Report ........................................ 1
    1.2    Format and Limitations ....................................... 2
            1.2.1   Differences in the Study Design ......................... 3
            1.2.2   Availability of Data ..................................... 3
    1.3    Historical Context of Bill C-15 ................................. 3
            1.3.1   Limitations of <u>Criminal Code</u> Provisions Prior to Bill C-15 .... 4
    1.4    Bill C-15: Goals, Objectives and Amendments .................... 8
            1.4.1   Goal # 1: To Provide Better Protection to Child Sexual
                     Abuse Victim/Witnesses ................................ 10
            1.4.2   Goal # 2: To Enhance Successful Prosecution of Child
                     Sexual Abuse Cases ................................... 11
            1.4.3   Goal # 3: To Improve the Experience of the Child
                     Victim/Witness ....................................... 11
            1.4.4   Goal # 4: To Bring Sentencing in Line with Severity of the
                     Offence ............................................. 12
            1.4.5   Research Strategy ..................................... 12

2.0 RESEARCH METHODOLOGY ..................................... 13

    2.1    Research Design ............................................. 13
    2.2    Study Components ........................................... 14
            2.2.1   Information Systems ................................... 14
            2.2.2   File Reviews .......................................... 15
            2.2.3   Court Observations .................................... 16

|  |  | 2.2.4 | Transcript Review | 17 |
|---|---|---|---|---|
|  |  | 2.2.5 | Key Informants Survey | 18 |
|  |  | 2.2.6 | Post Court Interviews | 18 |
|  | 2.3 | Measures and Operational Definitions | | 18 |
|  |  | 2.3.1 | Scale Development | 19 |
|  |  | 2.3.2 | Outcome Measures | 21 |

## 3.0 PROCESSING OF CHILD SEXUAL ABUSE CASES ............... 23

| | | | |
|---|---|---|---|
| 3.1 | Processing of Cases Through Parallel Systems | | 23 |
| 3.2 | Protocols and Procedures | | 25 |
| | 3.2.1 | Inter-agency Protocols | 25 |
| | 3.2.2 | Special Investigating Units | 26 |
| 3.3 | Parallel Processing of Cases: Case Overlap | | 26 |
| 3.4 | Processing of Cases in the Criminal Justice System | | 29 |
| | 3.4.1 | Criminal Justice System Case Profiles | 29 |
| | 3.4.2 | Criminal Justice System Case Rates | 33 |
| 3.5 | Decision Making in the Criminal Justice System | | 39 |
| | 3.5.1 | Decision to Lay Charges: Calgary | 42 |
| | 3.5.2 | Decision to Lay Charges: Edmonton | 42 |
| | 3.5.3 | Decision to Lay Charges: Hamilton | 43 |
| | 3.5.4 | Decision to Lay Charges: Saskatchewan | 43 |
| | 3.5.5 | Trends in the Decision to Lay Charges | 45 |
| 3.6 | Case Duration | | 45 |
| 3.7 | Child Victim/Witnesses in the Court Process | | 47 |
| | 3.7.1 | Overall Impression | 47 |
| | 3.7.2 | Child Victim/Witnesses in Court: Calgary | 48 |
| | 3.7.3 | Child Victim/Witnesses in Court: Edmonton | 49 |
| 3.8 | Summary | | 50 |
| | 3.8.1 | The Interrelationship Between the Child Welfare System and Criminal Justice System | 50 |
| | 3.8.2 | The Processing of Cases in the Criminal Justice System | 51 |

## 4.0 IMPLEMENTATION AND IMPACT OF BILL C-15, <u>AN ACT TO AMEND THE CRIMINAL CODE AND THE CANADA EVIDENCE ACT</u> .............. 55

| | | |
|---|---|---|
| 4.1 | Goal # 1: To Provide Better Protection to Child Sexual Abuse Victim/Witnesses | 55 |
| | 4.1.1 Objective # 1: To Broaden the Range of Conduct Captured by the <u>Criminal Code</u> | 55 |

|      |       |                                                                                                      |    |
|------|-------|------------------------------------------------------------------------------------------------------|----|
|      | 4.1.2 | Objective # 2: To Provide More Protection for Young Victims                                          | 65 |
|      | 4.1.3 | Objective # 3: To Eliminate Gender Bias Regarding Victims and Offenders                              | 67 |
|      | 4.1.4 | Objective # 4: To Provide Protection for Children in Cases Where Disclosure is Delayed               | 68 |
| 4.2  | Goal # 2: To Enhance Successful Prosecution of Child Sexual Abuse Cases                                      | 69 |
|      | 4.2.1 | Objective # 5: To Review the Problem of Child Sexual Abuse Victims Giving Evidence                   | 69 |
|      | 4.2.2 | Objective # 6: To Protect the Credibility of the Child Victim/Witness in Cases of Child Abuse        | 72 |
| 4.3  | Goal # 3: To Improve the Experience of the Child Victim/Witness                                              | 73 |
|      | 4.3.1 | Objective # 7: To Avoid Repetitious Interviews with the Child Victim/Witness                         | 73 |
|      | 4.3.2 | Objective # 8: To Provide Support and Assistance to the Child Victim/Witness While Giving Testimony  | 75 |
|      | 4.3.3 | Objective # 9: To Provide Protection for the Child Victim/Witness Regarding Identity and Circumstances of the Occurrence | 76 |
| 4.4  | Goal # 4: To Bring Sentencing in Line with the Severity of the Incident                                      | 78 |
|      | 4.4.1 | Objective # 10: To Provide for a Range of Sentence Responses to a Broad Range of Severity of Abuse   | 78 |
| 4.5  | Summary                                                                                                      | 82 |
|      | 4.5.1 | Goal # 1: To Provide Better Protection to Child Sexual Abuse Victim/Witnesses                        | 82 |
|      | 4.5.2 | Goal # 2: To Enhance Successful Prosecution of Child Sexual Abuse Cases                              | 82 |
|      | 4.5.3 | Goal # 3: To Improve the Experience of the Child Victim/Witness                                      | 83 |
|      | 4.5.4 | Goal # 4: To Bring Sentencing in Line with the Severity of the Offence                               | 83 |

**5.0 PERCEPTIONS OF PROFESSIONALS, CHILD VICTIMS AND PARENTS REGARDING BILL C-15, <u>AN ACT TO AMEND THE CRIMINAL CODE AND THE CANADA EVIDENCE ACT</u>** .............. 85

- 5.1 Perceived Problems With Substantive Sections of Bill C-15 ........ 85
  - 5.1.1 Issues Related to Specific Sections ...................... 86
- 5.2 Reported Experience With Procedural Items Related to Bill C-15 ................................................. 86
  - 5.2.1 Perceptions of Crown Prosecutors ....................... 87
  - 5.2.2 Perceptions of Defence Lawyers ........................ 88
  - 5.2.3 Perceptions of Judges ................................ 89
- 5.3 Perceived Changes Due to Bill C-15 ............................ 89
- 5.4 Impact Of Testifying On The Child ............................ 91
- 5.5 Effect of Bill C-15 On the Professionals ....................... 91
  - 5.5.1 Effects on The Job .................................. 91
  - 5.5.2 Policy ............................................ 92
  - 5.5.3 Training .......................................... 93
- 5.6 Perceptions Of Child Victim/Witnesses in Alberta ............... 93
  - 5.6.1 Court Preparation ................................... 93
  - 5.6.2 What Victim/Witnesses Would Tell Other Children ........ 94
  - 5.6.3 Testimony Experience ................................ 94
  - 5.6.4 General Comments About the Court Process .............. 95
- 5.7 Perceptions of Parents/Guardians in Alberta .................... 96
  - 5.7.1 Respondents ....................................... 96
  - 5.7.2 Social Workers ..................................... 96
  - 5.7.3 Police ............................................ 97
  - 5.7.4 Crown Prosecutors .................................. 97
  - 5.7.5 General Impact of Investigation/Reporting ............... 98
  - 5.7.6 Trial Information ................................... 98
  - 5.7.7 Post Court ........................................ 99
- 5.8 Summary ................................................. 100
  - 5.8.1 Perceived Problems with Substantive Sections of Bill C-15 ......................................... 100
  - 5.8.2 Reported Experience with Procedural Items Related to Bill C-15 ......................................... 100
  - 5.8.3 Perceived Changes Due to Bill C-15 .................... 100
  - 5.8.4 Impact of Testifying on the Child ...................... 101
  - 5.8.5 Effect of Bill C-15 on Professionals .................... 101
  - 5.8.6 Perception of Child Victim/Witnesses in Alberta .......... 101
  - 5.8.7 Perception of Parents/Guardians in Alberta ............. 101

## 6.0 CONCLUSIONS .... 103

- 6.1 The Interrelationship Between the Child Welfare System and the Criminal Justice System .... 103
  - 6.1.1 Protocols .... 103
- 6.2 The Experiences of the Child Victim/Witness in the Criminal Justice System .... 105
  - 6.2.1 Reporting Rates .... 105
  - 6.2.2 Case Profile .... 105
  - 6.2.3 Unfounded Rates .... 106
  - 6.2.4 Clearance Rates .... 106
  - 6.2.5 Conviction Rates .... 106
  - 6.2.6 Incarceration Rates .... 106
  - 6.2.7 Case Duration .... 107
  - 6.2.8 Child's Performance as a Witness .... 107
- 6.3 Impact of Bill C-15 .... 107
- 6.4 Achievement of the Goals .... 113
  - 6.4.1 Goal # 1: To Provide Better Protection to Child Sexual Abuse Victim/Witnesses .... 114
  - 6.4.2 Goal # 2: To Enhance Successful Prosecution of Child Sexual Abuse Cases .... 115
  - 6.4.3 Goal # 3: To Improve the Experience of the Child Victim/Witness .... 116
  - 6.4.4 Goal # 4: To Bring Sentencing in Line with the Severity of the Offence .... 116
- 6.5 Overview .... 117

## APPENDICES

Appendix A  Major Research Evaluation Reports on Child Sexual Abuse and the Impact of Bill C-15 .... 119

Appendix B  Tables and Figures .... 123

Appendix C  <u>Review and Monitoring of Child Sexual Abuse Cases in Selected Sites in Rural Alberta</u>: A Summary .... 143

## BIBLIOGRAPHY .... 149

# LIST OF FIGURES

| | | |
|---|---|---|
| Figure 3.1 | Child Sexual Abuse System Case Flow Model, Alberta and Ontario | 24 |
| Figure 3.2 | Types of Abuse for Substantiated Cases of Child Sexual Abuse By Location | 32 |
| Figure 3.3 | Reporting Rates of Child Sexual Abuse By Location and Year (Rate per 100,000 | 34 |
| Figure 3.4 | Flow of Child Sexual Abuse Cases Through the Criminal Justice System By Location | 36 |
| Figure 3.5 | Conviction Rates for Child Sexual Abuse By Location | 38 |
| Figure 3.6 | Conviction Rates for Child Sexual Abuse By Court Type and Location | 40 |
| Figure 3.7 | Incarceration Rates for Child Sexual Abuse By Location | 41 |
| Figure 3.8 | Decision Model for Cleared By Charge Cases of Child Sexual Abuse By Location | 44 |
| Figure 4.1 | Number of Charges under Specific Sections Relevant to Child Sexual Abuse in Calgary, Edmonton, and Saskatchewan from 1986 to 1990 | 57 |
| Figure 4.2 | Conviction Rates for Section 151 (Sexual Interference) By Location | 63 |
| Figure 4.3 | Conviction Rates for Section 271 (Sexual Assault) By Location | 64 |
| Figure 4.4 | Dispositions for Sections 151 and 271 in Calgary and Edmonton | 79 |
| Figure 4.5 | Incarceration Times for Sections 151 and 271 in Calgary and Edmonton | 80 |

# LIST OF TABLES

| | | |
|---|---|---|
| Table 1.1 | Criminal Code Number Transformations Relevant to the Assessment of Bill C-15 | 5 |
| Table 2.1 | Child Sexual Abuse Intrusion Levels and Nature of Abuse Categories | 20 |
| Table 3.1 | Child Welfare Agencies/Police Overlap of Child Sexual Abuse Cases by Location | 27 |
| Table 3.2 | Characteristics of Child Sexual Abuse Cases By Location | 28 |
| Table 3.3 | Average Elapsed Time Between First Occurrence, Most Recent Occurrence, Report to Police, Preliminary Inquiry and Trial, By Location | 46 |
| Table 4.1 | Range of Conduct for Cases Having Charges Under Sections 151, 152, 153 or 173(2) of the New <u>Criminal Code</u>, By Location | 59 |
| Table 4.2 | Issues Raised as Defence in Cross-Examination By Location | 74 |
| Table 4.3 | Courtroom Environment During the Child's Testimony | 77 |

# ACKNOWLEDGMENTS

The authors would like to acknowledge the assistance and cooperation of a number of people who made it possible to complete this report. First, we would like to thank Carolina Giliberti, the project manager at the Department of Justice Canada, and Hilary McCormack, Legal Counsel, Department of Justice Canada, for their guidance and comments throughout this project. Second, thanks are due to the project directors of the other site studies: Jane Campbell in Hamilton, and Greg Stevens and Don Fischer in Saskatchewan.

Finally, we are thankful for the support and hard work of the staff at the Canadian Research Institute for Law and the Family. Min Jong Won produced the graphics for the report, and Joanne Paetsch acted as project administrator and copy editor. Debra Perry and Janine Alison Isenegger also reviewed drafts of the report, and Beryl Parkinson competently and cheerfully produced numerous drafts on her word processor.

This research project was funded by the Department of Justice Canada. The Canadian Research Institute for Law and the Family is supported by a grant from the Alberta Law Foundation.

J.P.H.
F.B.
1992

# EXECUTIVE SUMMARY

## Introduction and Purpose of this Report

As part of a broad program of research and consultation, the Department of Justice Canada launched three major research evaluation projects to determine whether the goals and objectives of Bill C-15 were being realized in various locations across Canada. The first of these research initiatives, which began in August 1989, focussed on cases of child sexual abuse in Calgary, Edmonton and three rural locations in Alberta (see Hornick, Burrows, Perry and Bolitho, 1992, and Phillips and Hornick, 1992). The second study began in May 1990 and focussed on cases of child sexual abuse in Hamilton, Ontario (see Campbell Research Associates and Social Data Research Ltd., 1992). The third evaluation project began in November of 1990 and collected information on child sexual abuse cases in Regina and Saskatoon, Saskatchewan (see Fischer, Stevens and Berg, 1992).[1]

All three projects, although they were not identical, were designed to maximize comparability of study findings between the sites. The Alberta and Hamilton projects, for example, focussed on the following three distinct purposes:

(1) To describe the nature of the interrelationship between the child welfare system and the criminal justice system regarding child sexual abuse.

(2) To examine the nature of the child victim/witness experience in the criminal justice system since the proclamation of Bill C-15.

(3) To identify the degree to which the goals and objectives of Bill C-15 have been achieved.

The Saskatchewan study also focussed on the second and third study purposes, but did not include information concerning the child welfare system.

The purpose of this report is to summarize and compare the findings of the site studies conducted in Alberta, Saskatchewan, and Ontario to provide an overview of the extent to which various components of Bill C-15 have been implemented and the impact of the implementation.

---

[1] These reports are available on request from the Department of Justice Canada.

# Executive Summary

## Bill C-15, An Act to Amend the Criminal Code and the Canada Evidence Act

In 1980, concerns regarding the increase in the reported incidence of child sexual abuse led to the establishment of the Committee on Sexual Offences Against Children and Youths, chaired by Dr. Robin Badgley. The Committee gathered information on the incidence and prevalence of sexual offences against children in Canada and made recommendations for dealing with the problems identified. In all, the Committee made 52 recommendations directed at all levels of government, as well as the private sector. Many of the recommendations suggested improvement in the laws for the protection of children.

The federal government's response to the recommendations explicitly recognized two realities: (a) that an effective attack on the personal and social ills resulting from the sexual abuse of children required action by all levels of Canadian society; and (b) that leadership in this effort must come from the government of Canada. Thus, the federal government embarked on a course of action that involved the use of criminal law, as well as supporting social and educational reforms.

On October 15, 1986, the Honourable Ramon Hnatyshyn, then Minister of Justice and Attorney General of Canada, introduced Bill C-15 entitled "An Act to Amend the Criminal Code and the Canada Evidence Act," which was enacted by Parliament and received Royal Assent on June 30, 1987. Bill C-15 became law in Canada on January 1, 1988 (S.C. 1987, c-24, [now R.S.C. 1985, c.19 (3rd Supp.)]). By the proclamation of this Bill, the federal government sent a clear message that the protection of children and youths was a priority in Canada and that sexual abuse of children was unacceptable and would not be tolerated.

The design of amendments to the Criminal Code outlined in Bill C-15 were driven by four broad goals which were identified in the debates in the House of Commons. The official position stated as a broad policy statement was that the amendments to the Criminal Code should:

(1) provide better protection to child sexual abuse victim/witnesses;

(2) enhance successful prosecution of child sexual abuse cases;

(3) improve the experience of the child victim/witness; and

(4) bring sentencing in line with the severity of the offence.

Executive Summary

The overall strategy for accomplishing the above goals involved: (a) overall simplification of the law relating to sexual offences; (b) creation of new offences specific to acts of child sexual abuse; (c) changes regarding procedure and evidence; and (d) changes to the Canada Evidence Act regarding the testimony of child witnesses.

Simplification of the law involved legislative changes of several kinds. Some provisions were repealed completely (sections 141, 146, 151, 152, 153, 154 and 157 XCC). Other sections were rewritten to extend their protection to young males (sections 166 and 167 XCC) or to add additional provisions where the offence involved a child under the age of 18 (sections 155, 169 and 195 XCC). Three new offences were also created: sexual interference, invitation to sexual touching, and sexual exploitation (sections 151, 152 and 153 CC).

Changes regarding procedure and evidence included repealing the requirement for corroboration (section 274 CC); abrogating the doctrine of recent complaint (section 275 CC); extending the provisions excluding evidence concerning past sexual conduct and sexual reputation (subsection 276(1) and section 277 CC) to Bill C-15 offences; restricting publication of the identity of the complainant or a witness (subsection 486(3) CC); permitting testimony outside the courtroom (subsection 486(2.1) CC); and permitting the use of videotaped evidence (section 715.1 CC).[2] Finally, amendments to the Canada Evidence Act allow both victims and witnesses less than 14 years old to give sworn evidence if they understand the nature of the oath and are able to communicate the evidence. The amendments also make it possible for a child under 14 years old who does not understand the nature of the oath to give unsworn evidence if the child is able to communicate and "promises to tell the truth."

## Research Design

The study design and instruments for all the site studies were developed through a feasibility study funded by Health and Welfare Canada in cooperation with the Department of Justice Canada. Following the feasibility study, the first of the site studies examined child sexual abuse cases in Calgary, Edmonton and three rural Alberta locations. This study, conducted by the Canadian Research Institute for Law and the Family (CRILF), began in August 1989, approximately 19 months after the proclamation

---

[2] A number of these provisions (specifically sections 274, 275, 276(1), 277, and 486(3) CC) were enacted by Bill C-127, proclaimed August 4, 1982; however, they have been extended in provisions established by Bill C-15.

# Executive Summary

of Bill C-15. The Alberta study then provided a model for the other site studies. In May 1990, Campbell Research Associates implemented a very similar study design in Hamilton, Ontario, and the last study was implemented by Peat Marwick Stevenson & Kellogg in Regina and Saskatoon in November 1990.

Because of the planning and coordinating role of the Department of Justice Canada, the results from the various sites are, for the most part, directly comparable. The overall research design is briefly described below. The focus is on the common methodological elements among the three studies, rather than on the differences. Some minor variations in the specific components of the site studies do exist. Detailed descriptions of these differences are contained in the individual site reports.

All of the site studies began after Bill C-15 was proclaimed, thus a post test/longitudinal tracking study design was used. The exploratory nature of the studies, and the lack of an existing study model for assessing legislation, led to the development of a complex multi-component design. This design involved collecting data from numerous sources, utilizing a variety of data collection strategies. Initially six components were proposed. They included:

(1)　Analysis of existing information systems;

(2)　Review of agency files;

(3)　Direct observation of children in court;

(4)　Review of court transcripts;

(5)　Survey of key informants; and

(6)　Post court interviews with victims and/or guardians of victims.

Most of the design components were implemented successfully; however, the post court interviews of victims were difficult to obtain, especially if consent from the family had not been obtained prior to appearing in court. Thus it was determined that the completion of post court family interviews on a large scale was not feasible at any of the sites, and only a limited amount of information was obtained through this component.[3]

## Summary of Findings and Conclusions

The findings of the site studies are presented below as they relate to the three distinct research purposes discussed in the introduction. Conclusions relevant to the four broad policy goals of Bill C-15 are also presented.

### The Interrelationship Between the Child Welfare System and the Criminal Justice System[4]

#### Protocols

Consistent with the principle of "least intrusiveness" expressed in the Alberta Child Welfare Act (1985), complete investigations of allegations of child sexual abuse are required in Calgary and Edmonton by Alberta Family and Social Services only when the alleged offender is a family member. When the alleged perpetrator is not a family member (i.e., extrafamilial abuse), and protective services are determined unnecessary, the case may be referred directly to a community resource, because the child is not considered to be in need of protection.

While formal protocol in Alberta did not require inter-agency cooperation between police and Alberta Family and Social Services on all cases, there was evidence of considerable inter-agency cooperation for Calgary child sexual abuse cases when the offender lived with the child. Further, in Calgary, child welfare workers were the major source of referral of child sexual abuse cases to the police, and a considerable amount of case conferencing occurred. There was even more inter-agency involvement between the police and Alberta Family and Social

---

[3] The major exception to the implementation of the overall design was the rural component of the Alberta study. Because of the small number of cases and limited availability of data, the rural study depended on the case study method (see Phillips and Hornick, 1992).

[4] No information relevant to this section was collected in Saskatchewan.

Services in Edmonton than in Calgary. The nature of the cases that were involved was also different. Calgary Social Services focussed more on intrafamilial abuse cases, whereas the data suggest that Edmonton Social Services included a considerable proportion of extrafamilial abuse cases, reflecting a broader interpretation of the Alberta Family and Social Services mandate in Edmonton. In both Calgary and Edmonton, inter-agency committees with representatives from child welfare, police, and other relevant agencies have developed protocols to guide investigations of both physical and sexual abuse.

In Hamilton, suspected incidents of child sexual abuse were reported either to the police or to a Children's Aid Society (CAS). Regardless of who first received the report, the "Child Sexual Abuse Protocol" required the police and CAS agencies to inform each other of a possible offence. Because of their legislated mandate, CAS agencies were most concerned about intrafamilial cases of child sexual abuse. However, the Catholic Children's Aid Society tended to investigate all cases of abuse.

### Special Police Units

Edmonton Police Service, Calgary Police Service and the Hamilton-Wentworth Police Department all had specialized sex crime/child abuse units. In Edmonton and Hamilton, all cases of child sexual abuse were referred directly to these units. In contrast, complaints received by district offices in Calgary were often concluded by the police officer who answered the call, and were not usually referred to the special child abuse unit which is located at police headquarters.

### Overlap of Cases

As might be expected due to the variations in protocol, the overlap of active case files between child welfare agencies and police in Hamilton was very high (87 percent) in comparison with Calgary (41 percent) and Edmonton (48 percent).

## The Experiences of the Child Victim/Witness in the Criminal Justice System

### Reporting Rates

Reporting of alleged occurrences of child sexual abuse to police ranged from a low of 73 per 100,000 population for Hamilton in 1990 to a high of

158 per 100,000 population in 1989 for Saskatoon. Rates for the time periods of the various studies were relatively stable, except in Saskatoon where they increased significantly from 1988 to 1990. Overall, the reporting rates of child sexual assaults are high when compared to reporting rates for all sexual assaults, i.e., adults and children. This suggests that children are significantly over represented as victims of sexual assault.

Case Profile

Seventy to 80 percent of the victims from all sites were female. Age distribution was also consistent, with the exception of Edmonton where victims tended to be over 12 years old. In the other sites, victims tended to be under 12 years old and a significant proportion (15 to 22 percent) were under five years old.

The vast majority (i.e., over 94 percent) of the accused were male and most incidents were perpetrated on a female victim. Likewise, most accused were adults, but a significant number of accused were under 18 years old, particularly in Saskatchewan (29 percent). Overall, the majority of accused were not related to the victim. However, a significant proportion of accused (from a low of 30 percent for Saskatchewan to a high of 57 percent for Calgary) were fathers or other relatives. Edmonton had the largest proportion of accused who were strangers (25 percent), followed by Saskatchewan (16 percent), Hamilton (14 percent), and Calgary (five percent).

There was considerable consistency among the study sites in the type of abuse behaviour reported. The most common form was genital fondling, followed by oral sex. Vaginal penetration with the penis occurred in 11 percent (for Hamilton) to 20 percent (for Saskatchewan) of the cases.

Overall, there is considerable consistency among the study sites regarding case profiles. The few significant differences that do exist are likely due to differences in the protocol for recording and retaining information.

Unfounded Rates

Unfounded rates were generally low, ranging from seven percent in Edmonton to 22 percent for Hamilton cases.

False allegations (i.e., victim lied) as identified by police occurred in less that five percent of the total number of cases reported to police in Hamilton and less than two percent of the total number of cases reported in Calgary.

## Clearance Rates

Clearance by charge varied considerably across the study sites. Most of the variation, however, seems to be a function of record-keeping protocol and, therefore, caution should be exercised when using clearance rates as an indicator of police performance.

## Conviction Rates

Conviction rates for all charges of child sexual assault were significantly high in all jurisdictions (ranging from a low of 59 percent in Edmonton to a high of 83 percent in Hamilton). Controlling for the type of court, however, indicates that Youth Court, under the Young Offenders Act, had the highest rate of conviction. Provincial Court and Court of Queen's Bench (adult accused) had lower rates of conviction.

## Incarceration Rates

Overall, incarceration rates are consistent with previous research. They ranged from a low of 51 percent for Edmonton convictions to a high of 74 percent for Hamilton convictions.

## Case Duration

The average time duration from occurrence, to report to police, to trial ranged from a low of eight months for Edmonton cases to a high of 11 months for Hamilton cases.

## Child's Performance as a Witness

Because of the small number of cases, detailed analysis was limited to Calgary and Edmonton cases. However, the overall impressions of the court observers from all sites were very positive. They felt the child witnesses exhibited appropriate responses and coped well under stressful situations. The

# Executive Summary

detailed quantitative analysis of Calgary and Edmonton court observations and the child victim/witness interviews led to the following specific conclusions.

- Children who were physically harmed during the incident had more difficulty presenting evidence.

- Children had difficulty "telling the story" if a long period of time had passed.

- The fewer strangers in the courtroom and the more supportive adults, the easier it was for the child to give evidence.

- Cross-examination by defence lawyers was significantly the most stressful part of the court process.

- Child victim/witnesses' feelings about the court process (from post court interviews) seemed to be directly affected by the outcome of the proceedings. Victim/witnesses were more upset if the proceedings did not result in conviction.

## Impact of Bill C-15

The conclusions below are presented as they pertain to the impact of specific sections of Bill C-15. In this section, our intent is to point out which components of Bill C-15 are working and which are not.

### Section 150.1 (Consent No Defence)

Consent as a defence continued to be raised by defence lawyers in Calgary (48 percent of the cases reviewed), Edmonton (18 percent) and Saskatchewan (15 percent). However, it was not raised in any of the Hamilton cases. Where consent was raised, there was no evidence regarding whether or not it was accepted by the courts. Mistaken age was very seldom raised at any of the sites. Overall, the findings suggest that section 150.1 has been successfully implemented in the study sites.

### Subsection 150.1(2) (Consent and Age Difference)

This subsection was relevant only in a small number of cases in Calgary and Edmonton. Thus, conclusions cannot be drawn on the basis of the findings.

# Executive Summary

### Section 151 (Sexual Interference)

The findings from all study sites indicate substantial use of section 151. After section 271 (Sexual assault) it was the section under which charges were most frequently laid. Further, three sites (Calgary, Edmonton and Saskatchewan) reported increasing utilization of this section over time. This increase is associated with a decrease in the use of section 271 in Calgary and Saskatchewan.

Section 151 was used to cover a broad range of conduct in all study locations. Likewise, the pattern of conduct associated with charges under section 151 was consistent among the various study sites. The most frequently reported behaviour was genital fondling, followed by other types of fondling. Less than 15 percent of the cases charged under this section involved vaginal penetration with the penis.

There was a significant tendency to lay charges under both section 151 and section 271, particularly in Calgary. Further, in both Calgary and Hamilton, a significant number of section 151 charges were withdrawn. This could be an indication of plea negotiation or, alternatively, some Crown prosecutors may have preferred to proceed under the more tested section 271.

Conviction rates for section 151 were high in all jurisdictions, ranging from 52 percent to 80 percent. The high conviction rates, however, were due to a large extent to a high rate of guilty pleas, particularly in Edmonton and Saskatchewan, and high rates of charges withdrawn in Hamilton and Calgary. For those convicted, incarceration rates were 48 percent in Edmonton and 60 percent in Calgary. Further, the most common incarceration time in Calgary was low, with 50 percent receiving a sentence of three months or less, compared to 30 percent of the Edmonton cases receiving a sentence of three months or less.

The extensive use of section 151, the high conviction rates, and the application of the section to a broad range of behaviour all lead to the conclusion that section 151 has been fully implemented and is an appropriate, effective section.

### Section 152 (Sexual Invitation)

While significantly fewer charges were reported under section 152 than section 151, this is to be expected given the more specific application of this section. On the basis of limited data, however, it appears to have been used to

# Executive Summary

cover a broad range of conduct including invitation to touch and exposure, which are less intrusive conducts than those covered by section 151. Conviction rates were also significantly high. Overall, section 152 seems to be a useful and effective section, although it is by definition limited to certain types of conduct.

## Section 153 (Sexual Exploitation)

In all locations, few charges were reported under section 153. The fact that this charge is aimed at protection of the older victim (i.e., 15 to 18 years old) and, as well, is limited to accused who are in a position of authority or trust, may account for its limited application.

Despite the lack of application, an assessment of section 153, as well as sections 151 and 152, should not be conducted in isolation from the other sections. They are in reality a "set" of specific charges designed to cover a total range of situations, with section 151 being the broadest and section 153 being the most specific.

## Female Offenders (Sections 151, 152 and 153)

The small number of cases involving female offenders which went to disposition was somewhat unexpected since five percent of the cases investigated by police in Calgary and two percent of the cases investigated in Edmonton involved female suspects. However, most of these cases seem to be screened out prior to laying charges. If we consider only cases where the police have cleared by charge, this proportion drops to less than two percent both in Calgary (n=6) and Edmonton (n=9).

## Section 155 (Incest); Section 159 (Anal Intercourse); Section 160 (Bestiality); Section 170 (Parent/Guardian Procuring); Section 171 (Householder Permitting Sexual Activity); Section 172 (Corrupting Children)

The frequency of these offences was too low for any meaningful analysis. Either the conduct covered by these sections seldom occurs (as the data from these studies imply), or they are too difficult to enforce.

## Subsection 173(2) (Exposure to Children Under 14 years of Age)

Use of subsection 173(2) was infrequently reported. Calgary police, for example, laid only two charges under this section during the study. In Edmonton, where the section was most frequently used, charges were laid under this section when exposure was the only behaviour that occurred. When exposure occurred with other more serious behaviour, which it often did, police tended to lay charges under the more serious hybrid and indictable offence, and did not bother using this summary offence. Thus, although few charges were laid under this section and conviction tended to occur through guilty pleas (particularly in Edmonton), subsection 173(2) does seem to be useful for the "exposure only" summary offences.

Subsections 212(2) and (4) (Living On The Avails and Obtaining for Sexual Purpose Persons Under 18 Years Old)

During 1989, nine charges were laid under section 212 in Calgary. In 1990, the number decreased to five charges. In Edmonton, ten charges were laid under section 212 in 1989 and five in 1990. In Saskatchewan, only seven charges were laid under these sections and no charges were laid in Hamilton. Information on convictions was not available.

The number of charges under section 212 do not seem to reflect the real level of the problem of juvenile prostitution. The Calgary Police Commission Prostitution Report (1991) provides a probable explanation. This report documents that in 1988, 52 charges were laid under section 195.1 (Soliciting) against female prostitutes under 18 years old. In 1989, there were 57 charges under section 195.1 and the figure rose to 79 charges in 1990. The age of the female prostitutes charged under this section was as low as 13 years old. Unfortunately, comparable data were not available for any of the other sites. However, it is reasonable to assume that the trend of using section 195.1 to deal with female prostitution under 18 years of age would also hold.

The lack of use of subsections 212(2) and (4) and the continued use of section 195.1 is not consistent with the spirit of Bill C-15, i.e., the protection of the young. However, the objective of the use of section 195.1, according to the Calgary Police report, was to prevent the young person continuing to work as a prostitute (Calgary Police Commission Prostitution Report, 1991). With the help of the Justice of the Peace and the youth court judges, the youth have often been barred from the "stroll" areas of Calgary as a condition of release. Thus, the police seem to be applying the solicitation legislation simply because it is easier to enforce.

Further, anecdotal information obtained during the study and data from the professional survey suggest that subsection 212(2) (Living on the avails) is only enforceable when a prostitute turns against a pimp. Likewise, charges under subsection 212(4) (Obtaining a person under 18 years of age for sexual purposes) could only be enforced if the "John" was caught in the act. Thus, traditional policing methods do not seem to be appropriate for enforcement of subsections 212(2) and (4). Therefore, these sections have not been effective in dealing with the problem of juvenile prostitution.

### Section 271 (Sexual Assault)

As indicated in the discussion of section 151, section 271 is often used in combination with section 151. The impact of the use of section 271 in this study was impressive. The conviction rate was very high in all locations. Further, guilty pleas were high and rates of charges withdrawn were relatively low. The incarceration rates were also high. Overall, the results of the site studies indicate that section 271 is being used quite effectively to deal with child sexual assault in the criminal justice system.

### Section 272 (Sexual Assault, Level II, Sexual Assault, Level III)

The low frequency of these charges makes analysis impossible.

### Section 274 (Corroboration Not Required)

Such variables as the presence of more than one victim and the presence of a corroborative witness appeared to be important predictors in the decision by police to lay charges. However, they were not significant predictors of conviction at trial. This finding, along with the absence of any indication of concern regarding corroboration, seems to support the interpretation that the courts are considering section 274 seriously, since a considerable number of cases resulted in conviction without any type of corroboration.

### Section 275 (Recent Complaint Abrogated)

In the past, courts were permitted to allow into evidence statements made to a third party by the victim of a sexual assault. Section 275 abrogating this rule of recent complaint in sexual offences, which was first enacted in 1982 (Bill C-127), was extended to the new Bill C-15 sexual offences. No data were directly relevant to the abrogation of recent complaint.

### Subsection 276(1) (Sexual Activity)

Past sexual activities were very seldom raised as a defence in proceedings at any of the study sites. Thus, the absence of data to the contrary would suggest that this section has been implemented and was effective in child sexual abuse cases. This section, however, was struck down by the Supreme Court of Canada in August 1991 in R. v. Seaboyer; R. v. Gayme.

### Section 277 (Reputation Evidence)

Reputation as a defence was never raised in the cases studied in Calgary and Hamilton. However, it was raised in 18 percent of the Edmonton cases and four percent of the Saskatchewan cases. Perhaps the relative older age of the victims in Edmonton may account for the frequency at that location. The absence and relatively low occurrence of questions in proceedings concerning reputation evidence suggests that this section has also been relatively effective.

### Subsection 486(2.1) (Testimony Outside the Courtroom)

There was considerable variation among the study sites in relation to the implementation of subsection 486(2.1). For example, the screen was used in one-quarter of the cases observed in Saskatchewan, as well as nine percent of the cases in the Calgary courts. Hamilton courts, however, seldom used the screen at all. Saskatchewan courts were the only courts that used closed-circuit television (24 percent) during the time period of the study. The only other innovation used in a significant number of cases at all locations was support adults staying in the court. These data indicate that there are major problems with the adoption and implementation of this component of Bill C-15. Other innovations, however, were used.

### Subsection 486(3) (Order Restricting Publication)

Requests for a ban on publication were made in over 50 of the cases and were almost always ordered. Although this section predates Bill C-15, it is particularly relevant to sexual assault cases and is being used.

### Section 715.1 (Videotaped Evidence)

During the time period of the study, videotapes of the victim were made for 34 percent of the Saskatchewan cases, 18 percent of the Edmonton cases, three Calgary cases, and none of the Hamilton cases. Because of the R. v. Thompson (1989) judgement in Alberta, very few videotapes were actually used in court proceedings. While the R. v. Thompson judgement essentially blocked the implementation of this component of Bill C-15, it is interesting to note that Edmonton and Saskatchewan police continued to use videotaping as an investigative tool.

### Subsection 16(3) Canada Evidence Act (Oath)

Over three-quarters of the child victim/witnesses in Calgary and one-half of the child victim/witnesses in Edmonton were sworn. The rest gave testimony under the promise to tell the truth provision. In Hamilton, four of five child victim/witnesses were sworn. This provision seems to have been readily implemented and thus is facilitating children giving evidence.

### Additional Issue: Time Limitation

Prior to Bill C-15, section 141 provided that certain enumerated sexual offences could not be prosecuted if more than one year had elapsed from the time the alleged offence had occurred. This limitation was repealed by Bill C-15.

The repeal of this section was meant to protect children in situations where disclosure was delayed. For a small number of cases in this study, (i.e., six percent of the relevant cases in Calgary and two percent in Edmonton), disclosure was made more than one year after the incident and resulted in a 60 percent conviction rate in Calgary. A very high number of the relevant charges (77 percent) were also withdrawn in Calgary. However, problems prosecuting such cases could be due to difficulties the child might have had in remembering details of the offences.

### Achievement of the Goals

As indicated above, the amendments to the Criminal Code outlined in Bill C-15 were driven by four broad policy goals. The level to which these goals has been achieved reflects not only on the relative success of components of Bill C-15, but also on the appropriateness of the policy behind the bill. Therefore, the goals are reviewed below in light of the overall findings of the site studies.

### Goal # 1: To Provide Better Protection to Child Sexual Abuse Victim/Witnesses

The findings of this report strongly support the conclusion that the amendments outlined in Bill C-15 have provided better protection to child sexual abuse victim/witnesses. The specific findings which support this conclusion are listed below.

- There was a high degree of inter-agency cooperation in the development of protocols for dealing with child sexual abuse both in Ontario and Alberta.

- Calgary and Edmonton, Alberta, and Hamilton, Ontario police all had special child abuse investigation units.

- Reporting of alleged occurrences of child sexual abuse was high in all jurisdictions, ranging from a low of 73 per 100,000 in 1990 in Hamilton to a high of 158 per 100,000 in 1989 in Saskatoon.

- Children are significantly over represented as victims of sexual assault.

- Most victims were female under 12 years old and a significant number were under five years old (15 to 22 percent).

- A significant number (17 to 29 percent) of the accused were young offenders (12 to 17 years old).

- The number of charges under sections of Bill C-15 was high and increased over time. The number of charges laid under section 271 (Sexual assault) was also high.

- Conviction rates for most sections were high, especially if the accused was a young offender.

- Guilty plea rates were high, especially for section 271 (Sexual assault).

- A broad range of conduct was covered by section 151 (Sexual interference), section 152 (Sexual touching), section 153 (Sexual exploitation), and section 271 (Sexual assault).

- Many cases (20 to 30 percent) involve male victims and some female offenders were charged.

## Executive Summary

In addition to the above supportive findings, the following issues were identified:

- The lack of charges under subsection 212(2) (Living on the avails) and subsection 212(4) (Obtaining for sexual purposes) indicate that juvenile prostitutes were not helped by the new legislation.

- A significant proportion of substantiated cases did not conclude with charges being laid and subsequent conviction. Little is known about these cases. Further, if the cases involved an accused not related to the victim, the victim tended not to be followed up by the child welfare system.

### Goal # 2: To Enhance Successful Prosecution of Child Sexual Abuse Cases

The findings of this report generally support the conclusion that Bill C-15 procedural amendments have enhanced prosecution of child sexual abuse cases. The findings supporting this conclusion are listed below.

- In court proceedings, the child victim/witness was usually sworn, especially if they were over 12 years of age.

- If the child was not sworn, evidence was always taken under the promise to tell the truth.

- Corroboration was important for laying charges, but was not found to be related to conviction in trial.

- Some expert witnesses were being used, especially with younger children.

- Videotaping was found to be useful for police investigations and refreshing the child's memory prior to proceedings, as was the case in R. v. Beauchamp and Beauchamp.

The nonsupporting findings were as follows:

- R. v. Thompson limited the use of videotapes as evidence during the time of the site studies.

# Executive Summary

### Goal # 3: To Improve the Experience of the Child Victim/Witness

Assuming that all appearances in court as a victim of sexual assault are traumatic (whether the victim is an adult or a child), the findings of the site studies suggest that the changes due to Bill C-15, as well as other innovations, have improved the experience of the child victim/witness within the criminal justice system. The following findings led us to this conclusion.

- Ban on publication (subsection 486(3)) was widely used in all jurisdictions.

- The child victim/witness was usually allowed to turn away from the accused. In some jurisdictions, this was facilitated by the layout of the courtroom.

- Support adults were often present during court proceedings, and it was found that their presence made it easier for the child to give evidence.

- There is an openness on the part of judges, crown prosecutors, and defence lawyers to use innovative supports for children who are giving evidence.

In addition to the above supportive findings, a number of issues were identified and are listed below.

- Screens and closed-circuit television were seldom used.

- In the few cases where videotapes were used for evidence, the child was still extensively cross examined.

- Children had difficulty "telling the story" if a long period of time had passed since the incident.

- Cross-examination by defence lawyers was significantly the most stressful part of the court process for the child victim/witness.

### Goal # 4: To Bring Sentencing in Line with the Severity of the Offence

Unfortunately, sufficient data are not available to make any conclusions regarding this goal. Comparison and trend data are needed to reflect on the issue of adequacy of sentencing. The few relevant findings available are listed below.

- Incarceration rates for section 151 (Sexual interference) and section 271 (Sexual assault) ranged from 48 percent (for section 151 in Edmonton) to a high of 62 percent (for section 271 in Calgary).

- Time of incarceration for section 271 was slightly higher than for section 151 (section 151 = 6.7 months in Calgary and 11.1 months in Edmonton compared to section 271 = 9.9 months in Calgary and 11.2 months in Edmonton).

## Overview

The impact of Bill C-15 can be summarized as follows:

- The substantive components of Bill C-15 are providing better protection to children who have been sexually abused.

- The procedural components of Bill C-15 are contributing to successful prosecution of child sexual abuse cases.

- The use of innovations during court proceedings improves the experience of the child victim/witness.

We are confident in concluding that most aspects of Bill C-15 are working well, and that the professionals involved have adapted to and accepted the changes. We wish to stress, however, as our data indicate, that the scope and complex nature of the problem of child sexual abuse requires a response far broader than a legal response alone.

# 1.0 INTRODUCTION: LEGISLATIVE RESPONSE TO CHILD SEXUAL ABUSE

Public awareness and concern about the problem of child sexual abuse have rapidly increased since the mid-1970s (Finkelhor, 1986).[1] The number of cases reported to agencies, the number of professionals involved, and the literature on the subject have also grown throughout this period. In Canada, both the child welfare system and the criminal justice system are mandated to respond to reports of child sexual abuse. The circumstances of a particular occurrence determine whether one or both systems become involved. The criminal justice system is empowered to investigate all cases of child sexual assault regardless of the relationship of the offender to the victim. In contrast, the child welfare system becomes involved primarily in cases where either a child is considered to be at substantial risk of being sexually abused by a guardian or the guardian cannot or is unwilling to protect the child from abuse.

Both systems have recently attempted to respond to the problem of child sexual abuse. The most far reaching of these responses was the proclamation on January 1, 1988, of Bill C-15, <u>An Act to Amend the Criminal Code and the Canada Evidence Act</u>. This Act contained a number of major revisions to substantive and procedural laws governing the sexual abuse of children. It also contained a "review clause" (see Bill C-15, section 19), requiring that the Bill be reviewed after four years.

## 1.1 Purpose of this Report

As part of a broad program of research and consultation, the Department of Justice Canada launched three major research evaluation projects to determine whether the goals and objectives of Bill C-15 were being realized in various locations across Canada. The first of these, which began in August 1989, focussed on cases of child sexual abuse in Calgary, Edmonton and three rural locations in Alberta (see Hornick, Burrows, Perry and Bolitho, 1992, and Phillips and Hornick, 1992). The second study began in May 1990 and focussed on cases of child sexual abuse in Hamilton, Ontario (see Campbell Research Associates and Social Data Research Ltd., 1992). The third evaluation project began in

---

[1] Throughout this report "child sexual abuse" and "child sexual assault" are used to refer to incidents or occurrences of sexual assault on a victim under 18 years old.

November of 1990 and collected information on child sexual abuse cases in Regina and Saskatoon, Saskatchewan (see Fischer, Stevens and Berg, 1992).[2]

All three projects, although they were not identical in method and scope, were designed to maximize comparability of study findings between the sites. The Alberta and Hamilton projects, for example, focussed on the following three distinct purposes:

(1) To describe the nature of the interrelationship between the child welfare system and the criminal justice system regarding child sexual abuse.

(2) To examine the nature of the child victim/witness experience in the criminal justice system since the proclamation of Bill C-15.

(3) To identify the degree to which the goals and objectives of Bill C-15 have been achieved.

The Saskatchewan study also focussed on the second and third study purposes, but did not include information concerning the child welfare system.

The purpose of this report is to summarize and compare the findings of the site studies conducted in Alberta, Saskatchewan, and Ontario to provide an overview of the extent to which various components of Bill C-15 have been implemented and the impact of the implementation.

## 1.2  Format and Limitations

The report is organized as follows:  Chapter 1.0 outlines the specific goals and objectives of Bill C-15; Chapter 2.0 briefly outlines the methodology of the study; Chapter 3.0 presents the findings relevant to the processing of child sexual abuse cases through the child welfare and criminal justice systems and presents information about child victim/witness behaviour in the court process; Chapter 4.0 presents findings relevant to the specific objectives of Bill C-15; Chapter 5.0 presents findings on the perceptions of police, Crown prosecutors, defence lawyers, judges, and social workers on their role in the processing of cases, as well as perceived problems with both the substantive and procedural aspects of Bill C-15; and Chapter 6.0 presents the conclusions.

---

[2] These reports, listed in Appendix A, are available on request from the Department of Justice Canada.

To the extent possible, this report focusses on information common to all three site studies. However, differences in the nature of the various site studies, as well as regional differences in the availability of data, impose certain limitations on the comparisons made in this report. These limitations are briefly described below.

### 1.2.1 Differences in the Study Design

Both the Saskatchewan and Ontario studies began after the Alberta study, and were conducted over shorter time frames. While file information was available for similar periods of time, only a limited amount of time was available for court observation of children giving testimony, resulting in a smaller number of cases. Further, the Saskatchewan study team was not contracted to collect data from child welfare files. Thus, comparisons in this area can only be made between Alberta and Ontario.

### 1.2.2 Availability of Data

Variations in agency protocol for recording and storing information directly affects the availability and comparability of data. For example, Regina police protocol involved classifying cases of child sexual abuse cleared without laying charges as "other," with no reference to sexual abuse, making it difficult to track these cases. Such limitations are referred to in the text of this report.

## 1.3 Historical Context of Bill C-15

In 1980, concerns regarding the increase in the reported incidence of child sexual abuse led to the establishment of the Committee on Sexual Offences Against Children and Youths, chaired by Dr. Robin Badgley. The Committee gathered information on the incidence and prevalence of sexual offences against children in Canada and made recommendations for dealing with the problems identified. In all, the Committee made 52 recommendations directed at all levels of government, as well as the private sector. Many of the recommendations suggested improvement in the laws for the protection of children (Report of the Committee on Sexual Offences Against Children and Youths, 1984).

The federal government's response to the recommendations explicitly recognized two realities: (a) that an effective attack on the personal and social ills resulting from the sexual abuse of children required action by all levels of Canadian society; and (b) that leadership in this effort must come from the government of Canada. Thus, the federal government embarked on a course of action that involved the use of criminal law, as well as supporting social and educational reforms.

On October 15, 1986, the Honourable Ramon Hnatyshyn, then Minister of Justice and Attorney General of Canada, introduced Bill C-15 entitled "<u>An Act to Amend the Criminal Code and the Canada Evidence Act</u>," which was enacted by Parliament and received Royal Assent on June 30, 1987. Bill C-15 became law in Canada on January 1, 1988 (S.C. 1987, c-24, [now R.S.C. 1985, c.19 (3rd Supp.)]). By the proclamation of this Bill, the federal government sent a clear message that the protection of children and youths was a priority in Canada and that sexual abuse of children was unacceptable and would not be tolerated.

### 1.3.1 Limitations of Criminal Code Provisions Prior to Bill C-15

The first step in amending the <u>Criminal Code</u> to better protect children was to critically review the sexual offences in the Code prior to January 1, 1988 which were relevant to child sexual abuse. Table 1.1 identifies the relevant sections of the <u>Criminal Code</u> prior to Bill C-15, indicating which sections were repealed or carried over to the new <u>Criminal Code</u>, as well as amendments and new provisions added by Bill C-15.

While we do not intend to discuss each section of the old Code sections listed, it is useful to summarize some of the inadequacies of the old provisions regarding the protection of children. Among the limitations of the <u>Criminal Code</u> that have been identified are the following:

- Gender Bias

Girls and boys were given different protection by the law. In many offences, the victim had to be female and the accused male. For example, although step-fathers and foster fathers committed a crime if they had sexual intercourse with their step-daughters or foster daughters, the same prohibition did not apply to step-mothers with step-sons or foster sons. Also, only females could be victims of the seduction offences and only males could be the offenders.

- Limited Range of Sexual Activity

Some offences prohibited only vaginal sexual intercourse and did not encompass the range of sexual activities that could constitute child abuse, such as fondling, masturbation and oral intercourse by the child on the offender from which both girls and boys should be protected.

## Table 1.1   Criminal Code Number Transformations Relevant to the Assessment of Bill C-15[1]

| \multicolumn{2}{c}{Old Criminal Code Prior to Jan. 1, 1988} | Interim Code (C-15) | \multicolumn{2}{c}{New Criminal Code as of Jan. 1, 1988} | |
|---|---|---|---|---|
| XCC | Section Description | | CC | Section Description |
| s. 140 | Consent no defence | s. 139 | s. 150.1 | Consent no defence |
| s. 141 | Time limitation (repealed 1987) | | | |
| s. 146(1) | Sexual intercourse with female under 14 years (repealed 1987) | | | |
| s. 146(2) | Sexual intercourse with female between 14-16 years of previous chaste character (repealed 1987) | | | |
| | | s. 140 | s. 151 | Sexual interference for children under 14 |
| | | s. 141 | s. 152 | Invitation to sexual touching for children under 14 |
| | | s. 146 | s. 153 | Sexual exploitation for children 15-18 |
| s. 150 | Incest - Intercourse with a blood relative | s. 150 | s. 155 | Incest |
| s. 151 | Seduction of a female 16-18 years old of previous chaste character (Repealed 1987) | | | |
| s. 152 | Seduction of a female under 21 years old under promise of marriage (Repealed 1987) | | | |
| s. 153 | Sexual intercourse with stepdaughter/foster daughter (Repealed 1987) | | | |
| s. 154 | Seduction of a female passenger on vessels (Repealed 1987) | | | |
| s. 155 | Buggery or bestiality (Repealed 1987) | s. 154 | s. 159 | Anal intercourse |
| | | s. 155 | s. 160 | Bestiality |
| s. 157 | Gross indecency (Repealed 1987) | | | |
| s. 166 | Parent/guardian procuring sexual activity (Repealed 1987) | s. 166 | s. 170 | Parent/guardian procuring sexual activity |
| s. 167 | Householder permitting sexual activity (Repealed 1987) | s. 167 | s. 171 | Householder permitting sexual activity |
| s. 168 | Corrupting children (Repealed 1987) | s. 168 | s. 172 | Corrupting children |
| s. 169 | Indecent act | s. 169(1) | s. 173(1) | Indecent Act |
| | | s. 169(2) | s. 173(2) | Exposure to child under 14 years |

## Table 1.1 (continued)[1]

| Old Criminal Code Prior to Jan. 1, 1988 | | Interim[2] Code (C-15) | New Criminal Code as of Jan. 1, 1988 | |
|---|---|---|---|---|
| XCC | Section Description | | CC | Section Description |
| s. 195(1) | Procuring | s. 195(1) | s. 212(1) | Procuring |
| s. 195(2) | Living off avails (repealed 1987) | s. 195(2) | s. 212(2) | Living off avails of a prostitute under 18 years |
| | | s. 195(4) | s. 212(4) | Obtaining person under 18 years for sexual purpose |
| s. 195.1 | Soliciting | s. 195.1 | s. 213 | Soliciting |
| s. 246.1 | Sexual assault | s. 246.1 | s. 271 | Sexual assault |
| s. 246.2 | Sexual assault with a weapon/threats/bodily harm | s. 246.2 | s. 272 | Sexual assault with a weapon/threats/bodily harm |
| s. 246.3 | Aggravated sexual assault | s. 246.3 | s. 273 | Aggravated sexual assault |
| s. 246.4 | Corroboration not required | s. 246.4 | s. 274[3] | Corroboration not required |
| s. 246.5 | Rules re: recent complaint abrogated | s. 246.5 | s. 275[3] | Rules re: recent complaint abrogated |
| s.246.6(1) | No evidence concerning sexual activity | s. 246.6(1) | s. 276(1)[3] | No evidence concerning sexual activity |
| s. 246.7 | Reputation evidence | s. 246.7 | s. 277[3] | Reputation evidence |
| | | s. 442(2.1) | s. 486(2.1) | Testimony outside the court room |
| s. 442(3) | Order restricting publication | s. 442(3) | s. 486(3)[3] | Order restricting publication |
| | | s. 643.1 | s. 715.1 | Videotaped evidence |
| CEA s.16 | Sworn/unsworn evidence of a child (repealed 1987) | CEA s. 16 | s. 16 | Child witness oath/promise to tell truth |

---

[1] Throughout this report old code numbers (XCC) will be used when the old code (prior to January 1, 1988) is referred to. When the new code is referred to the new code numbers (CC) will be used and interim code numbers (Bill C-15) will be ignored.

[2] The interim code numbers were introduced with Bill C-15. They related to new sections introduced by Bill C-15 and, in addition, include sections carried over from the old Criminal Code. The interim codes were used for approximately one year.

[3] These sections were enacted by Bill C-127 (August 1982), however, they were extended to the sexual offences enacted by Bill C-15.

- Requirement of Previous Chaste Character

Girls who had been sexually active and/or sexually abused in the past could not be considered of "previously chaste character" and therefore could not be protected. Victims of such sexual abuse could well be in need of more protection from the law rather than less, after the first forcible acts of sexual intercourse.

- Victim's Sexual Reputation and Activity Used as Defence

Proving the defence that the accused is "not more to blame" than the victim required cross-examination of the victim's sexual reputation and past sexual activity. To many observers and to women's groups, this was often seen as unjust. They believed that victims were being victimized a second time by a legal system that permitted such tactics.

- Presumption that a Male Under 14 was Incapable of Intercourse

The legal presumption in the <u>Criminal Code</u> that a boy under 14 years is incapable of sustaining a penile erection and engaging in sexual intercourse is no longer consistent with biological reality. This level of maturity now occurs in boys at least as young as 12, which is also the age of criminal responsibility. Under the former law, youths under 14 could not be held criminally responsible for acts of sexual intercourse with girls under 14 or for such acts committed in an incestuous relationship.

- Issues Regarding Age and Consent

The age of legal consent varied, depending on the particular sexual act and the sex of the participant. A male could consent to sexual intercourse at any age. A female of 14 years or more could consent to vaginal intercourse. Neither sex could consent to acts of anal intercourse or gross indecency until age 21, with the exception that a female could marry at age 16 and then consent to such acts with her husband.

- Invitation to Sexual Touching

Sexual assault legislation prior to Bill C-15 did not make it an offence for a person to invite a child to touch him or her in a sexual way. In surveying the incidence of sexual abuse, the Badgley Committee found this to be a common type of activity.

- Time Restrictions

Under sexual assault legislation prior to Bill C-15, certain sexual offences had to be prosecuted within a year after their commission. Many children have difficulty talking about such experiences, and delayed disclosure often precluded the prosecution of sexual offences against children.

## 1.4 Bill C-15: Goals, Objectives and Amendments

The design of amendments to the Criminal Code outlined in Bill C-15 were driven by four broad goals which were identified in the debates in the House of Commons. The official position stated as a broad policy statement was that the amendments to the Criminal Code should:

(1) provide better protection to child sexual abuse victim/witnesses;

(2) enhance successful prosecution of child sexual abuse cases;

(3) improve the experience of the child victim/witness; and

(4) bring sentencing in line with the severity of the offence.

The overall strategy for accomplishing the above goals involved: (a) overall simplification of the law relating to sexual offences; (b) creation of new offences specific to acts of child sexual abuse; (c) changes regarding procedure and evidence; and (d) changes to the Canada Evidence Act regarding the testimony of child witnesses.

Simplification of the law involved legislative changes of several kinds (see Table 1.1). Some provisions were repealed completely (sections 141, 146, 151, 152, 153, 154 and 157 XCC). Other sections were rewritten to extend their protection to young males (sections 166, and 167 XCC) or to add additional provisions where the offence involved a child under the age of 18 (sections 155, 169 and 195 XCC). Three new offences were also created: sexual interference, invitation to sexual touching, and sexual exploitation (sections 151, 152 and 153 CC). As a result of these changes, there are now twelve sexual offences in the Criminal Code which are applicable to cases of child sexual abuse:

(1)  Sexual assault;

(2)  Sexual interference;

(3) Invitation to sexual touching;

(4) Sexual exploitation;

(5) Indecent acts and indecent exposure;

(6) Incest;

(7) Anal intercourse;

(8) Bestiality and associated offences;

(9) Parent or guardian procuring sexual activity;

(10) Householder permitting sexual activity;

(11) Living off avails of a prostitute under 18 years; and

(12) Obtaining a person under 18 years for sexual purpose.

Changes regarding procedure and evidence included repealing the requirement for corroboration (section 274 CC); abrogating the doctrine of recent complaint (section 275 CC); extending the provisions excluding evidence concerning past sexual conduct and sexual reputation (subsection 276(1) and section 277 CC) to Bill C-15 offences; restricting publication of the identity of the complainant or a witness (subsection 486(3) CC); permitting testimony outside the courtroom (subsection 486(2.1) CC); and permitting the use of videotaped evidence (section 715.1 CC).[3] Finally, amendments to the Canada Evidence Act allow both victims and witnesses less than 14 years old to give sworn evidence if they understand the nature of the oath and are able to communicate the evidence. The amendment also makes it possible for a child under 14 years old, who does not understand the nature of the oath, to give unsworn evidence if the child is able to communicate and "promises to tell the truth."

Although there was not a one-to-one correspondence between the strategies promoted by the legislation (as discussed above) and the four general goals of Bill C-15, the logical linkages are obvious. In the absence of a clear statement of these linkages, the first task of the research team was to identify and

---

[3] A number of these provisions (specifically sections 274, 275, 276(1), 277, and 486(3) CC) were enacted by Bill C-127 proclaimed August 4, 1982; however, they have been extended in provisions established by Bill C-15.

clearly articulate these linkages. Thus, below, specific changes made by Bill C-15 are linked to the specific goals by expected outcome or objectives. These objectives will then provide the basis for the specific research questions which must be answered in order to assess the impact of Bill C-15.

### 1.4.1 Goal # 1: To Provide Better Protection to Child Sexual Abuse Victim/Witnesses

The amendments relating to this goal can be viewed as falling into four areas of expected outcome. First, the repeal of subsection 146(1) XCC (Intercourse with a female under 14 years) and subsection 146(2) XCC (Intercourse with a female 14 to 16 years) and the replacement of these sections with section 151 CC (Sexual interference), section 152 CC (Invitation to sexual touching), and section 153 CC (Sexual exploitation), are presumed to have at least two intended outcomes: (a) broadening the range of conduct captured by the Criminal Code; and (b) eliminating gender bias regarding victims and offenders.

Second, the proclamation of section 150.1 CC (Consent of child under 14 years old no defence), subsection 173(2) CC (Exposure to a child under 14 years old), subsection 212(2) CC (Living on the avails of a prostitute under 18) and subsection 212(4) CC (Obtaining a person under 18 years old for sexual purpose) are presumed to be aimed at providing more protection for young victims.

Third, the repeal of section 141, which provided a one-year limitation period for certain sexual offences, and the abrogation of the doctrine of recent complaint with respect to all sexual offences (section 275 CC), was aimed at protecting children in cases where disclosure was delayed.

Thus, the expected outcomes associated with the amendments relevant to Goal # 1 are expressed as the following objectives:

Objective # 1:   To broaden the range of conduct captured by the Criminal Code.

Objective # 2:   To provide more protection for young victims.

Objective # 3:   To eliminate gender bias regarding victims and offenders.

Objective # 4:   To provide protection for children in cases where disclosure is delayed.

### 1.4.2 Goal # 2: To Enhance Successful Prosecution of Child Sexual Abuse Cases

The amendments related to Goal # 2 fall into two areas. First, section 715.1 CC, permitting admission in evidence of a videotape of the victim's description of events, and subsection 16(1) of the <u>Canada Evidence Act</u>, allowing victims/witnesses under 14 years old to give testimony under oath or on a promise to tell the truth, facilitate the giving of evidence by children. Second, removal of the requirement for corroboration under section 274 CC for charges related to child sexual abuse, and exclusion of evidence of sexual activity (subsection 276(1) CC) and reputation (section 277 CC) of the victims are presumed to be an attempt to eliminate previous impediments to the credibility of the child victim/witness.

The expected outcomes associated with the amendments relevant to Goal # 2 are expressed as the following objectives:

Objective # 5: To minimize the problems of the child sexual abuse victim giving evidence.

Objective # 6: To recognize the credibility of the child victim/witness in child sexual abuse cases.

### 1.4.3 Goal # 3: To Improve the Experience of the Child Victim/Witness

This particular goal is broader than the other goals; however, some of the amendments of Bill C-15 are relevant. First, the proclamation of section 715.1 CC, which permits the use of videotape of the victim's description of events, is intended to avoid repetitious interviews with the child victim/witness. The videotape can also be used to support a child's testimony by allowing the child to refresh his or her memory by viewing the tape both prior to and during proceedings. Second, support and assistance can be provided to the child victim/witness through the exclusion of the public from the courtroom by subsection 486(1) CC.[4] Third, support can be provided by subsection 486(2.1), which permits the child witness to testify outside the courtroom or behind a screen. Fourth, subsection 486(3), which provides for a ban on publication of the identity of the witness, can be viewed as providing protection to the child

---

[4] Section 486(1) predates Bill C-15 but as this provision is particularly applicable to sexual offences the extent of its use was also analyzed in this report.

victim/witness by preventing broad public knowledge of the child's identity and the circumstances of the occurrence.

The expected outcomes associated with the amendments relevant to Goal # 3 above are expressed as the following objectives:

Objective # 7: To avoid repetitious interviews with the child victim/witness.

Objective # 8: To provide support and assistance to the child victim/witness while giving testimony.

Objective # 9: To provide protection to the child victim/witness from public knowledge of the child's identity and the circumstances of the occurrence.

### 1.4.4 Goal # 4: To Bring Sentencing in Line with Severity of the Offence

Consistent with the fact that the new legislation is designed to cover a broad range of behaviour, most of the sections (specifically sections 151, 152, 153, 159, and 160 CC) are hybrid offences, ensuring that the range of sentencing alternatives is also broad. The expected outcome associated with the amendments relevant to Goal # 4 can be expressed as the following objective:

Objective # 10: To provide for a range of sentence responses to a broad range of severity of abuse.

### 1.4.5 Research Strategy

Given the expected outcomes of Bill C-15 expressed as Objectives 1 to 10 above, the strategy for assessing the impact of the new legislation involved investigating two basic questions:

(1) Are the new sections being used?

(2) When the new sections are being used, are the desired outcomes being achieved?

We return to these two generic questions regarding the achievement of the specific objectives of Bill C-15 in Chapter 4.0 of this report.

## 2.0 RESEARCH METHODOLOGY

The study design and instruments for all the site studies were developed through a feasibility study funded by Health and Welfare Canada in cooperation with the Department of Justice Canada. Following the feasibility study, the first of the site studies examined child sexual abuse cases in Calgary, Edmonton and three rural Alberta locations. This study, conducted by the Canadian Research Institute for Law and the Family (CRILF), began in August 1989, approximately 19 months after the proclamation of Bill C-15. The Alberta study then provided a model for the other site studies. In May 1990, Campbell Research Associates implemented a very similar study design in Hamilton, Ontario, and the last study was implemented by Peat Marwick Stevenson & Kellogg in Regina and Saskatoon in November 1990.

Because of the planning and coordinating role of the Department of Justice Canada, the results from the various sites are, for the most part, directly comparable. The overall research design, instruments, and operational definitions are briefly described below. Focus is on the common methodological elements among the three studies, rather than on the differences. Some minor variations in the specific components of the site studies do exist. Detailed descriptions of these differences are contained in the individual site reports.

### 2.1 Research Design

All of the site studies began after Bill C-15 was proclaimed, making it impossible to implement a pretest/post test design. Instead, a post test/longitudinal tracking study design was used. The exploratory nature of the studies, and the lack of an existing study model for assessing legislation, led to the development of a complex multi-component design. This design involved collecting data from numerous sources, utilizing a variety of data collection strategies. Initially six components were proposed. They included:

(1)   Analysis of existing information systems;

(2)   Review of agency files;

(3)   Direct observation of children in court;

(4)   Review of court transcripts;

(5)   Survey of key informants; and

(6)  Post court interviews with victims and/or guardians of victims.

Most of the design components were implemented successfully; however, the post court interviews of victims were difficult to obtain, especially if consent from the family had not been obtained prior to appearing in court. Thus it was determined that the completion of post court family interviews on a large scale was not feasible at any of the sites, and only a limited amount of information was obtained through this component. Comprehensive results from the remaining study components are presented in this report.[1]

## 2.2 Study Components

### 2.2.1 Information Systems

Agency data from computerized information systems were available only for the Alberta sites.

#### Sample: Calgary and Edmonton

Alberta Family and Social Services (AFSS) provided a computer listing from their Child Welfare Information System (CWIS). The listing contained all the investigations completed between January 1, 1988 and July 31, 1990 where the investigation outcome was designated as a form of child sexual abuse. The cases consisted of both intrafamilial and extrafamilial situations where a parent or guardian was unwilling or unable to protect a child from sexual abuse and/or exploitation. Between January 1, 1988 and July 31, 1990, the CWIS system reported 801 active cases involving child sexual abuse in Calgary and 1148 cases in Edmonton.

The Calgary and Edmonton municipal police departments also provided computer data regarding police reports involving child sexual abuse allegations. In Calgary data were obtained from the Police Information Management System (PIMS), and in Edmonton the Records and Criminal Intelligence Analysis System (CIA) was used. The police data indicated 1556 cases were investigated in Calgary and 1736 cases were investigated in Edmonton. Police investigations

---

[1] The major exception to the implementation of the overall design was the rural Alberta study. Because of the small number of cases and limited availability of data, the rural study depended on the case study method (see Phillips and Hornick, 1992).

resulted in 997 specific charges being laid in Calgary and 674 charges being laid in Edmonton.

In cases where criminal charges were laid, the names of the accused were searched in the Attorney General's information system (Criminal Justice Information System (CJIS)) by viewing records on terminal screens at the two police departments. This was done to determine outcomes or dispositions for cases that were processed through the court system. The number of police reports, the number of cases in which criminal charges were laid, and the final disposition data, provide an overview or tracking of child sexual assault cases in the criminal justice system. Disposition data were available from CJIS for 89 percent of the charges in Calgary and 83 percent of the charges in Edmonton.

### 2.2.2 File Reviews

Two file review forms were developed to gather specific information from the various files. First, the Child Welfare File Review Form facilitated the collection of general case information, information regarding the case profile and history, an assessment of the child victim, a description of the victim's family and, if possible, information regarding the alleged offender. Second, the Police File Review Form was developed to collect general case information for each incident involving a child victim and an alleged perpetrator of sexual assault. Information regarding the report to the police, the subsequent investigation, the police decision to lay charges, and the use of specialized investigative procedures such as videotaping, was also collected by the researchers.

<u>Samples: Calgary and Edmonton</u>

File reviews were conducted on 244 child welfare cases from Calgary, 396 cases from Edmonton, and 53 cases from the Alberta rural areas. All of these files involved cases in which charges had been laid by police and/or the child welfare investigation outcome was child sexual abuse during the period January 1, 1988 to July 31, 1989.

In terms of police file information, 731 files were reviewed in Calgary, 655 in Edmonton, and 43 from the rural areas. The Calgary sample included all the cases identified in the log books where charges were laid from January 1, 1988 to July 31, 1990, and all cases cleared otherwise or not cleared from August 1, 1989 to July 31, 1990. Due to the large volume of cases and time restrictions, the Edmonton data consisted of all charged cases for the entire study period and a 20 percent random sample of cases between August 1, 1989 and July 31, 1990 where charges were not laid.

Sample: Hamilton

All child sexual abuse cases reported to the Catholic Children's Aid Society and the Hamilton-Wentworth Children's Aid Society for the period September 1, 1989 to August 31, 1990 were reviewed. This included 400 allegation reports to these child welfare agencies. Likewise, all occurrences of child sexual abuse reported to Hamilton-Wentworth police for the period September 1, 1989 to August 31, 1990 were tracked and reviewed. This procedure resulted in a total sample of 325 victim/occurrence reports being reviewed.

Sample: Saskatchewan

For the period January 1, 1988 to December 31, 1990, a total of 1101 police files from Saskatoon and Regina were reviewed and included in the study. This sample included all occurrences of child sexual abuse reported to Saskatoon police (n=738), regardless of how the case was cleared. Child welfare files were not reviewed in Saskatchewan, in accordance with their contract.

### 2.2.3 Court Observations

Court observations were conducted to collect first-hand information on the nature and quality of a child's testimony, as well as the overall effect of the court experience on the child. A general observation checklist was used to describe the type of court proceedings and components of the process, such as the use of screens, videotaped evidence, etc. Individual rating scales developed from the work of Achenbach and Edelbrock (1983) and Goodman (1988) were also utilized to describe the child's behaviour and verbal abilities at each of the three stages of testimony: (a) determining the child's ability to take an oath or communicate (when necessary); (b) the examination in chief; and (c) cross-examination.

Sample: Calgary and Edmonton

A total of 74 child victim/witnesses were observed at preliminary inquiry and 80 were observed at trial. Victim/witnesses were often observed during a number of proceeding stages. This included 73 individual children from Calgary and 54 from Edmonton. In total, 197 preliminary inquiry and 235 trial observation forms were filled out in Calgary and Edmonton. Only two court observations were conducted in the rural locations.

Sample: Hamilton

Due to a delay in approving the protocol and other implementation problems beyond the control of the researchers, only 11 children were observed in court in Hamilton. These 11 cases provided data for 23 preliminary inquiry observations and 11 trial observations.

Sample: Saskatchewan

In Saskatchewan, 51 observations were completed, 38 during preliminary inquiries and 13 during trials. Ten were conducted during the oath stage, 19 during examination-in-chief, 19 during cross-examination, and three during re-examination.

### 2.2.4 Transcript Review

The Court Proceedings Review Forms were used to collect information from transcripts or audiotapes of preliminary inquiries and trials for cases within the criminal justice system. The review provided information regarding the types of charges, how children were treated as witnesses, the procedures utilized, the legislation followed, and other specific details of the court process.

Sample: Calgary and Edmonton

During the study, 23 preliminary inquiry transcripts were reviewed in Calgary and 49 in Edmonton. In addition, eight trial transcripts were reviewed.

Sample: Hamilton

Because transcripts or audiotapes of court proceedings are not normally made in the Hamilton-Wentworth district, only seven were available to the researchers. Only three of these cases involved child victim/witnesses who had not previously been observed directly in court.

Sample: Saskatchewan

In Saskatchewan, a total of 105 preliminary inquiry transcripts or audiotapes were reviewed. Thirty-five trial transcripts were also completed during the time of the study.

### 2.2.5 Key Informants Survey

A mailed survey technique was utilized to obtain perceptions and information covering Bill C-15 from key informants. Key informants consisted of the professionals involved in processing cases in the child welfare and criminal justice systems, such as child welfare workers, police, defence lawyers, crown prosecutors, and judges (see Appendix B, Table B-1).

<u>Sample: Calgary and Edmonton</u>

The return rates range from a high of 78 percent for police to a low of 34 percent for judges.

<u>Sample: Hamilton</u>

Return rates for the professionals in Hamilton ranged from a high of 46 percent for crown prosecutors to a low of 14 percent for defence lawyers.

<u>Sample: Saskatchewan</u>

In Saskatchewan, the highest return rate was 86 percent for police. The lowest return rate was 20 percent for defence lawyers.

### 2.2.6 Post Court Interviews

As indicated previously, the implementation of the post court interviews with victims and/or parents was not very successful, and thus does not warrant detailed exposition in this report. In total, only seven victims and seven parent/guardians from Calgary and Edmonton were interviewed. In Hamilton, five child victim/witnesses and four parents were interviewed. In Saskatchewan, only three parent interviews were completed, and these were dropped from the report due to the small amount of data.

## 2.3 Measures and Operational Definitions

Analysis of the data of these studies required the development of several scales and the operationalization of various outcome measures. The development of these scales and measures are discussed below.

### 2.3.1 Scale Development

An extensive literature review indicated that most of the current research regarding severity of sexual abuse has focussed on the resulting trauma of adults and children as the main indicator of the seriousness or severity of a childhood sexual abuse experience.[2] This process appears to have been utilized mostly for therapy purposes. Research that is specific to child victims and includes a multivariate analysis of factors describing the severity or seriousness of an abuse occurrence is sparse. How this information relates to decision making by social workers, teachers, police, judges or individuals working with children disclosing sexual abuse is not clear.

The current site studies focussed specifically on the nature of the behaviour manifested. When conceptualizing sexual abuse as a combination of behavioural events, the 20 categorical variables listed in Table 2.1 were used. When it was necessary to conceptualize the abuse behaviour as a continuous concept, the intrusion levels shown in Table 2.1 were used.

---

[2] See Hornick, Burrows, Perry and Bolitho (1992) for a summary of this review.

### Table 2.1   Child Sexual Abuse Intrusion Levels and Nature of Abuse Categories

| Code | Intrusion Levels | Code | Nature of Abuse Categories |
|---|---|---|---|
| 1 | Exposure | 1 | Exposure |
| 2 | Invitation | 2 | Invitation |
|  |  | 3 | Show Pornography |
|  |  | 4 | Undress |
| 3 | Masturbation | 5 | Masturbation |
| 4 | Innapropriate Kissing | 6 | Inappropriate Kissing |
| 5 | Non-Genital Fondling | 7 | Chest Fondling |
|  |  | 8 | Buttock Fondling |
| 6 | Genital Fondling | 9 | Genital Fondling |
| 7 | Mutual Genital Fondling | 10 | Victim Fondling Offender |
| 8 | Simulated Intercourse | 11 | Sexual Activity with Others |
|  |  | 12 | Simulated Intercourse |
| 9 | Digital Penetration | 13 | Vaginal Penetration with Finger |
|  |  | 14 | Attempted Vaginal Penetration |
|  |  | 15 | Anal Penetration with Finger |
| 10 | Oral Sex | 16 | Oral Sex on Offender |
|  |  | 17 | Oral Sex on Victim |
| 11 | Vaginal Penetration with Penis | 18 | Vaginal Penetration with Penis |
| 12 | Anal Penetration with Penis | 19 | Anal Penetration with Penis |
| 13 | Forced Prostitution | 20 | Forced Prostitution |

### Child Behaviour in Proceedings

Since one of the purposes of these studies was to examine the nature of the child's experience in court proceedings, the Court Observation Rating Scales were developed from the previous work of Achenbach and Edelbrock (1983) and Goodman (1988). The nature of "child behaviour ratings" and the "child communication" items required the development of summated scales.

Factor analysis of all 29 child behaviour related items yielded three distinct subscales -- Anxious/Withdrawn, Sad/Cries, and Able to Communicate that achieved acceptable levels of reliability (see Appendix B, Table B-2).

Analysis required the development of an overall indicator of child performance throughout various court proceedings. Thus, scale scores were tested for change according to the stage of proceedings. This analysis indicated that oath taking tended to produce relatively low levels of Anxious/Withdrawn behaviour, particularly in comparison with cross-examination. None of the differences for Sad/Cries behaviour were significant. Ability to Communicate, however, decreased during cross-examination.

### 2.3.2 Outcome Measures

A number of outcome/performance measures were relevant to these studies and will be referred to when discussing the findings of this report. These concepts are briefly detailed below.

### Reporting Rate

Reporting rate is the total number of occurrences (both unfounded or substantiated, see below) reported to police per 100,000 population.

### Unfounded Rate

Unfounded incidents are the reports that are identified as false, or unable to prove, by the police during their preliminary investigation. The proportion of unfounded cases to cases where the incident is believed to have happened (i.e., substantiated) is the unfounded rate.

### Clearance Rate

The clearance rate is the proportion of substantiated occurrences that are cleared by the police laying charges. Cases not "cleared by charge" are either "cleared otherwise" (e.g., not enough evidence to proceed, offender cannot be identified) or they are classified as "not cleared." Cases not cleared consist mainly of cases where the investigation is continuing.

## Conviction Rate

Conviction rate is computed by dividing the number of charges that result in a guilty plea or conviction in court by the total number of guilty pleas, convictions, acquittals and charges discharged. Since this rate is considered the performance indicator for the crown prosecutor, only charges which are pursued by the crown are included. Cases for which charges are withdrawn, pending, stayed, or for which a warrant has been issued are not considered when determining the conviction rate. As Loh (1980) points out, there is no inherently correct baseline for comparison of conviction rates. However, the use of complaint and arrest rates can be misleading since a high proportion of cases are screened out before they are presented for charging.

## 3.0 PROCESSING OF CHILD SEXUAL ABUSE CASES

This chapter focusses on the processing of child sexual abuse cases through the child welfare and criminal justice systems. Most of the data analysis in this chapter is exploratory and descriptive. The information obtained is most relevant to the first two purposes of the studies, specifically:

(1) to describe the nature of the interrelationship between the child welfare and criminal justice systems regarding child sexual abuse; and

(2) to examine the nature of the child victim/witness experience with the criminal justice system since the proclamation of Bill C-15.[1]

### 3.1 Processing of Cases Through Parallel Systems

The case flow model shown in Figure 3.1 has been developed to organize the issues to be examined in these studies. This model includes the key events, major decisions and processes that may occur as child sexual abuse cases are dealt with by the child welfare or criminal justice system.

The model is organized according to the specific stages of the process for each system. For the child welfare system, the cases proceed through the following specific stages: (a) report; (b) investigation; (c) investigation outcome; (d) case status decision; (e) court proceedings; and (f) proceedings outcome. In comparison, the criminal justice system and stages generally consist of: (a) report; (b) investigation; (c) investigation outcome; (d) clearance; (e) plea by offender; (f) court proceedings; and (g) disposition.

Obviously not all cases proceed through either entire system. A screening process results in only a proportion of the cases proceeding through each stage. This screening process is affected by the policies and protocols of each system, which are briefly outlined below.

---

[1] In accordance with their contract, the Saskatchewan research team did not collect information on child welfare cases. Therefore, Saskatchewan data will not be included in some sections of this chapter.

**Figure 3.1  Child Sexual Abuse System Case Flow Model, Alberta and Ontario**

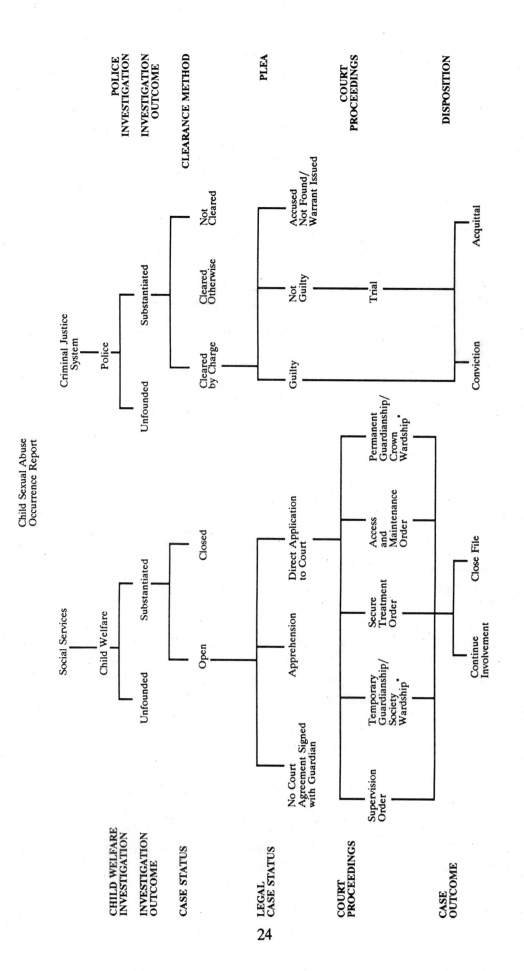

* Alberta terminology/Ontario terminology

## 3.2 Protocols and Procedures

### 3.2.1 Inter-agency Protocols

Specific child sexual abuse reporting and investigation protocols were established in Calgary, Edmonton, Hamilton and rural Alberta. However, there are differences in the nature and implementation of the protocols among the various sites.

The <u>Alberta Child Welfare Act</u> was revised effective July 1, 1985, to reflect the provincial government's belief in autonomy of the family unit. Subsection 1(2) states a child is in need of protective services "...if there are reasonable and probable grounds to believe that ... (d) the child has been or there is substantial risk that the child will be physically injured or sexually abused by the guardian of the child; (e) the guardian of the child is unable or unwilling to protect the child from physical injury or sexual abuse" (p. 5). The Child Welfare Handbook and Program Manual (Alberta Family and Social Services, 1989) includes guidelines for police involvement in child welfare investigations. Situations where a child has probably been sexually abused or exploited must be reported to the police. Once a report is made, the manner in which a joint investigation is conducted is determined by the professionals involved.

In both Calgary and Edmonton, specific investigation protocols have been developed by an inter-agency committee consisting of representatives from the municipal police department, child welfare and treatment services in the community. The responsibilities of each department and the case management and investigative procedures are outlined in the document (Alberta Family and Social Services, 1987).

In the Calgary and Edmonton regions, cases that are reported to the police first are often, but not always, then reported to child welfare. In cases of extrafamilial sexual abuse (i.e., cases involving an alleged perpetrator who is a stranger, employer, day care worker, etc.), the police may deal with the investigation alone. The child welfare system focusses on intrafamilial abuse and usually does not become involved with extrafamilial cases unless the parent or guardian appears to be unable to protect a child from sexual exploitation.

In Hamilton, a suspected incident of child sexual abuse is reported either to the police or to one of the Children's Aid Societies (CAS). As outlined in the "Child Sexual Abuse Protocol," police and CAS agencies are obligated to inform each other of a possible offence. Because of the legislated mandate of CAS under the <u>Child and Family Services Act</u> (S.O.,1984, c.55), the child welfare agencies are most concerned about intrafamilial cases of child sexual abuse. However, the Catholic Children's Aid Society investigates all allegations reported to them, whether intra or extrafamilial abuse. The Children's Aid Society, in contrast, tends to concentrate on the intrafamilial cases.

### 3.2.2 Special Investigating Units

The Edmonton Police Service, Calgary Police Service and Hamilton Wentworth Regional Police all have specialized sex crimes/child abuse units and detectives that investigate reported occurrences of sexual abuse of children. The sex crimes/child abuse unit of the Edmonton Police Service and Hamilton Police are responsible for investigating all cases of child sexual abuse in their jurisdiction and is located at police headquarters. In contrast, Calgary Police Service has two units, the child abuse unit and the sex crimes unit, which handle most investigations of child sexual abuse. However, complaints received at the district offices are often investigated and concluded locally -- thus, neither the cases nor file information on these cases are processed through one of the special units which are located at police headquarters.

### 3.3   Parallel Processing of Cases:  Case Overlap

This section presents information on the "overlap" of active files between the police agencies and the child welfare agencies. The data were obtained from the information systems or paper files of the various agencies; therefore, the sample includes the theoretical total population of cases.[2] Data on overlap were available for Calgary, Edmonton and Hamilton. The Saskatchewan study, however, did not review child welfare files, therefore, similar information is not available from that location.

Table 3.1 indicates that the proportion of overlap ranges from a low of 41 percent for Calgary to a high of 87 percent for Hamilton. Further analysis of the overlap data presented in Table 3.2 suggests an explanation for the relatively low rates of overlap for the Alberta sites. Note first that, in Calgary, cases cleared by charge by the police tended to also have child welfare files. The

---

[2] Note, however, that the Alberta Child Welfare Information System (CWIS) included only cases with an investigation outcome of sexual abuse rather than those reported for suspected sexual abuse. Thus, cases designated as unfounded at initial investigation were not included. This limitation required re-analysis of the Hamilton data with the exclusion of unfounded cases.

importance of being charged also holds, to a less significant degree, with Edmonton cases, but is not significant for Hamilton cases.

Next, Table 3.2 documents the importance of the relationship of the accused to the victims, particularly for the Alberta sites. Note that in cases which have both a police file and a child welfare file, the accused tends to be a family member, or member of the household (i.e., for Calgary 46 percent of the cases compared to 13 percent having no child welfare file; likewise, for Edmonton 55 percent compared to 28 percent; and for Hamilton 36 percent compared to five percent). Conversely, in all locations, cases which do not overlap tend to be those in which the accused is a stranger, particularly for the Alberta locations (i.e., 52 percent for Calgary, 34 percent for Edmonton, and 39 percent for Hamilton).

**Table 3.1** **Child Welfare Agencies/Police Overlap of Child Sexual Abuse Cases by Location[1]**

|   |   | Calgary[2] | Edmonton[2] | Hamilton[3] |
|---|---|---|---|---|
| A | Child Welfare Agencies Number of Cases | 513 | 760 | 284 |
| B | Number of Victims on Police and Child Welfare Records | 209 | 362 | 248 |
| C | Overlap | 40.7% | 47.6% | 87.3% |

---

[1] The unit of analysis is victim/occurrence.
Time period for Calgary and Edmonton is January 1, 1988 - July 31, 1990 (31 months).
Time period for Hamilton is September 1, 1989 - August 31, 1990 (12 months).

[2] Child Welfare files existed only for those cases which had an investigation outcome designated as a form of sexual abuse. Thus, cases reported for sexual abuse and designated unfounded were not included.

[3] The total number of cases here was 471. However, cases unfounded by child welfare workers were removed (n=187) in order to achieve a more reliable comparison with the Alberta sites.

## Table 3.2 Characteristics of Child Sexual Abuse Cases By Location

| Characteristic | Calgary[1] | | | | Edmonton[1] | | | | Hamilton[2] | | | |
| --- | --- | --- | --- | --- | --- | --- | --- | --- | --- | --- | --- | --- |
| | Police Case Without Child Welfare File | | Police Case With Child Welfare File | | Police Case Without Child Welfare File | | Police Case With Child Welfare File | | Police Case Without Child Welfare File | | Police Case With Child Welfare File | |
| | n | % | n | % | n | % | n | % | n | % | n | % |
| **Case Status** | | | | | | | | | | | | |
| Substantiated Cases | | | | | | | | | | | | |
|   Cleared by Charge | 482 | 36.2 | 144 | 64.6 | 306 | 21.7 | 110 | 32.0 | 16 | 20.8 | 62 | 25.0 |
|   Cleared Otherwise | 268 | 20.1 | 43 | 19.3 | 171 | 12.1 | 66 | 19.2 | 31 | 40.3 | 111 | 44.8 |
|   Not Cleared | 467 | 35.0 | 23 | 10.3 | 833 | 59.2 | 142 | 41.3 | 15 | 19.5 | 18 | 7.3 |
| Sub-total | 1217 | 91.3 | 210 | 94.2 | 1310 | 93.0 | 318 | 92.4 | 62 | 80.5 | 191 | 77.0 |
| Unfounded Cases | 116 | 8.7 | 13 | 5.8 | 98 | 7.0 | 26 | 7.6 | 15 | 19.5 | 57 | 23.0 |
| **Total** | 1333 | 100.0 | 223 | 100.0 | 1408 | 100.0 | 344 | 100.0 | 77 | 100.0 | 248 | 100.0 |
| **Relationship of Accused to Victim** | | | | | | | | | | | | |
|   Babysitter | | | | | 42 | 4.2 | 14 | 7.6 | | | | |
|   Unknown (Stranger) | 695 | 52.1 | 41 | 18.4 | 340 | 34.1 | 13 | 7.0 | 30 | 39.0 | 15 | 6.0 |
|   Known (Acquaintance) | 471 | 35.3 | 80 | 35.9 | 326 | 32.7 | 55 | 29.7 | 37 | 48.1 | 101 | 40.7 |
|   Family[3] | 167 | 12.6 | 102 | 45.7 | 277 | 27.8 | 102 | 55.1 | 4 | 5.2 | 88 | 35.5 |
|   Relative | | | | | | | | | 5 | 6.5 | 36 | 14.5 |
|   Other | | | | | | | | | 1 | 1.3 | 8 | 3.2 |
|   Not Recorded | | | | | 13 | 1.3 | 1 | 0.5 | | | | |
| **Total[4]** | 1333 | 100.0 | 223 | 100.0 | 998 | 100.0 | 185 | 100.0 | 77 | 100.0 | 248 | 100.0 |

[1] Time period for Calgary and Edmonton is January 1, 1988 - July 31, 1990 (31 months)

[2] Time period for Hamilton is September 1, 1989 - August 31, 1990 (12 months)

[3] Family includes "Members of Household"

[4] This information is not available in the Edmonton Police Records System, only on the CIA system. Therefore, for Edmonton, the total number of cases is smaller than that for case status.

The relatively low rate of overlap of active cases and the increased importance of the accused being a family member for the Alberta sites is consistent with the principle of least intrusion expressed by Alberta child welfare legislation. In contrast, as discussed in Section 3.2 above, it is the practice of child welfare agencies, particularly the Catholic Children's Aid Society in Ontario, to investigate all allegations of sexual abuse reported to them, whether it is considered intrafamilial or extrafamilial abuse.

## 3.4 Processing of Cases in the Criminal Justice System

In this section, information is presented on the characteristics and number of cases of child sexual abuse that have been processed through the criminal justice system.[3] Relevant rates are discussed and the "screening" process is documented from initial report to police, through prosecution by the crown to disposition.

### 3.4.1 Criminal Justice System Case Profiles

Characteristics of the victims, accused and occurrences are briefly outlined below and comparisons are made among the various sites. All the information in this section has been taken from the police file reviews.

<u>Victims</u>

The vast majority of victims were female in all sites. The largest proportion of female victims was 83 percent for Edmonton cases, and the lowest was 72 percent for Hamilton cases. There was also considerable consistency among the sites in terms of the distribution of age of the victim at the time of the report, with the exception of Edmonton cases, which tended to involve older victims (56 percent of Edmonton victims were over 12 years old compared to 49 percent for Calgary, 37 percent for Hamilton and 31 percent for Saskatchewan). Therefore, younger victims under four years old were under represented in Edmonton. Less than five percent of Edmonton victims were under four years old, compared to 15 percent for Calgary, 18 percent for Hamilton, and 22 percent for Saskatchewan.

---

[3] Child sexual abuse was operationally defined as all cases involving a victim who is under 18 years of age in an occurrence which could result in charges under any of the sections of the <u>Criminal Code</u> listed in Table 1.1.

Accused Characteristics

For all sites, the accused was male in the vast majority of cases (i.e., over 94 percent). Further, most incidents of abuse involved a male perpetrator and a female victim (i.e., 79 percent for both Calgary and Saskatchewan, and 84 percent for Edmonton). Incidents involving male victims and male offenders also occurred frequently. The least frequent occurrences involved female victims and female offenders.

Most of the accused were adults when the report was made to police (i.e., 83 percent for Calgary and Hamilton cases, 82 percent for Edmonton cases and 71 percent for Saskatchewan cases). However, there was a significant number of accused under 18 years old, particularly in Saskatchewan (29 percent).

In terms of the relationship of the accused to the victim, the largest proportion of intrafamilial cases was found in Calgary with 57 percent of the accused being father figures (33 percent) or relatives (24 percent). Hamilton cases also had a significant proportion of fathers (24 percent) and other relatives (16 percent). Edmonton cases, however, had fewer fathers (18 percent) and relatives (13 percent), as did Saskatchewan cases (fathers=14 percent; relatives=16 percent). Edmonton cases had the largest proportion of accused who were strangers (25 percent), followed by Saskatchewan (16 percent), Hamilton (14 percent), and Calgary (five percent).

Occurrence Characteristics

Victims from all sites most often disclosed to their mothers (48 percent for Calgary, 38 percent for Edmonton, 37 percent for Hamilton, and 33 percent for Saskatchewan). Friends ranked second for Calgary cases (10 percent) and Edmonton cases (12 percent), while social workers ranked second for disclosures in Hamilton (12 percent) and Saskatchewan (12 percent). The majority of cases were also reported within one month of the last incident. However, a significant number of cases were reported immediately after the incident (i.e., 13 percent for Calgary, 53 percent for Edmonton, 20 percent for Hamilton, and 28 percent for Saskatchewan), or more than one year after the last incident (i.e., 19 percent for Calgary, 11 percent for Edmonton, 14 percent for Hamilton, and 15 percent for Saskatchewan). The majority of occurrences involved only one accused (i.e., 90 percent for Calgary, 93 percent for Edmonton, 97 percent for Hamilton, and 86 percent for Saskatchewan), however, Saskatchewan had the largest relative percentage of multiple offender cases (14 percent).

The duration of abuse sometimes lasted over one year in all locations (26 percent of Calgary cases, 14 percent of Edmonton cases, and 14 percent of

Saskatchewan cases). However, the majority of cases involved single incidents (i.e., 36 percent of Calgary cases, 58 percent of Edmonton cases, and 45 percent of Saskatchewan cases). As Figure 3.2 indicates, the most common form of behaviour reported in all locations was genital fondling which occurred in 46 percent of the Hamilton cases, 45 percent of the Saskatchewan cases, 25 percent of the Calgary cases, and 22 percent of the Edmonton cases. Oral sex also often occurred (18 percent of Calgary cases, 12 percent of Edmonton cases, 18 percent of Hamilton cases, and 23 percent of Saskatchewan cases). Vaginal penetration with the penis occurred in 16 percent of the Calgary cases, 14 percent of the Edmonton cases, 11 percent of the Hamilton cases, and 20 percent of the Saskatchewan cases.

Additional witnesses, usually corroborative, were involved in almost one-third of the cases (31 percent for Calgary and Edmonton, 28 percent for Hamilton, and 24 percent for Saskatchewan). Expert witnesses were used far less frequently (nine percent of Calgary cases, four percent of Edmonton cases, and 13 percent of Saskatchewan cases).

Enticement was used in approximately ten percent of the cases in Calgary, Edmonton and Hamilton. Alcohol was also used in ten to 20 percent of the cases. Being physically forced to cooperate was most frequently reported in Saskatchewan occurrences (36 percent), however, it was also frequently reported by the other sites (i.e., 17 percent for Calgary cases, 29 percent for Edmonton cases, and 16 percent for Hamilton cases). Weapons were reported in less than four percent of the cases, however physical injury was reported in approximately ten percent of the cases (i.e., 12 percent in Calgary, ten percent in Edmonton, and 12 percent in Saskatchewan). Emotional injury, as reported by police, occurred in 40 percent of the Calgary cases, 18 percent of the Edmonton cases, and 12 percent of Saskatchewan cases.

**Figure 3.2** Types of Abuse for Substantiated Cases of Child Sexual Abuse By Location

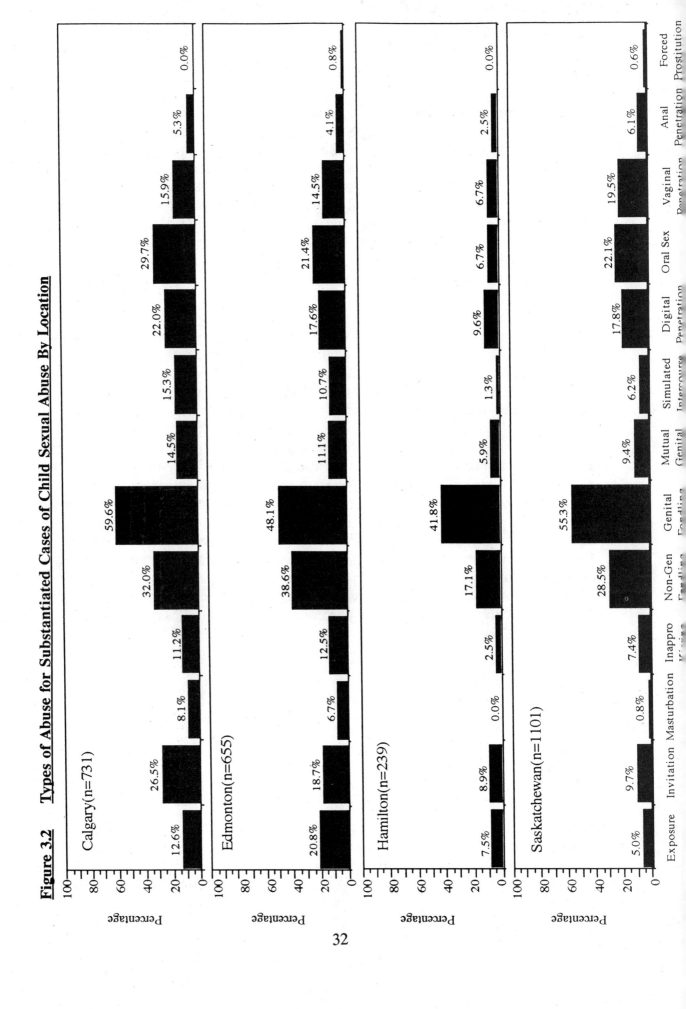

### 3.4.2 Criminal Justice System Case Rates

#### Reporting Rates[4]

Figure 3.3 contains the rates of reporting alleged occurrences of child sexual abuse to police from the various study sites. These rates range from a low of 73 per 100,000 population for Hamilton in 1990 to a high of 158 for Saskatoon in 1990. Rates over time increased significantly only in Saskatoon, where they rose from 90 per 100,000 in 1988 to 158 in 1990. The rates for Calgary and Edmonton remained relatively stable over time. The rate for one rural location in Alberta, i.e., Gleichen, was significantly higher than the urban locations in Alberta at 139 per 100,000. These rates are significantly high when compared to the reporting rates for all sexual assaults. In 1988, for example, the sexual assault reporting rate for all victims (i.e., children and adults) was 146 per 100,000 in Alberta, 103 per 100,000 in Saskatchewan, and 104 per 100,000 in Ontario (Roberts, 1990b). These findings seem to support the argument that a significant proportion of the incidents of sexual assault are perpetrated on child victims.

#### Overall Flow of Cases

Once cases of child sexual abuse are reported to the police, a decision-making process begins and cases are filtered into various categories and subcategories. Figure 3.4 provides a picture by location, of this decision-making process from the time cases of child abuse were reported until they were processed through the criminal justice system. Overall, it is obvious that only a portion of cases actually flow through all steps of the system. Unfortunately, differences in the units of analysis and missing data make it impossible to reliably track all cases through the system. Therefore, analysis of these data focusses on the individual steps throughout the process and is presented below.

---

[4] The Regina police used a different protocol for record keeping than any other police department in these studies. This protocol involved classifying child sexual abuse cases where no charge was laid as "other," with no reference to sexual abuse or assault. This resulted in an over representation of cases cleared by charge in Regina and deflated reporting rates. Thus, Regina data is omitted from the analysis here.

**Figure 3.3** **Reporting Rates of Child Sexual Abuse By Location and Year (Rate per 100,000)[1,2,3]**

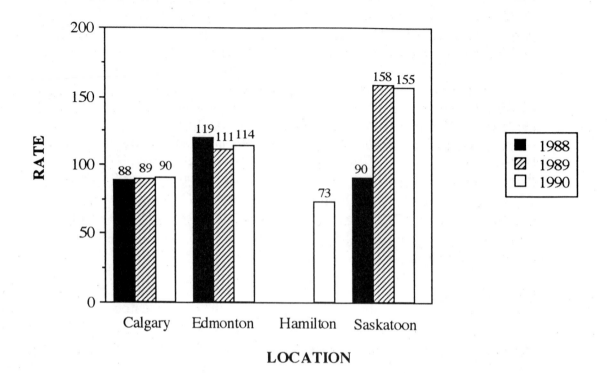

---

[1] The population of Calgary was: 1988 = 657,118; 1989 = 671,138 and 1990 = 692,885.
The population of Edmonton was: 1988 = 576,249; 1989 = 583, 872 and
1990 = 605,538.
The population of Hamilton was: 1990 = 447,600.
The population of Saskatoon was: 1988 = 183,487; 1989 = 183,896 and 1990 - 183,579.

[2] The time period for Calgary and Edmonton is January 1, 1988 - July 31, 1990
(31 months).
The time period for Hamilton is September 1, 1989 - August 31, 1990 (12 months).
The time period for Saskatchewan is January 1, 1988 - December 31, 1990 (36 months).

[3] Regina rates are deflated due to record keeping protocol and thus are omitted here.

Unfounded Rates

As Figure 3.4 indicates, there is a considerable amount of variation in the proportion of cases classified as unfounded across the study sites. The unfounded rate was lowest for Saskatoon at less that five percent, and highest for Hamilton at 22 percent. Calgary and Edmonton were similar at eight percent and seven percent respectively. These figures are comparable to the average unfounded rate of 15 percent for all sexual assaults for the period 1983 to 1988 (Roberts, 1990b).

Some data from the police file reviews were available on why the police classified occurrences as unfounded. The major reason given was "lack of evidence." This was the reason given for 75 percent of the Calgary unfounded cases, as well as 65 percent of the Hamilton cases and 48 percent of the Edmonton cases. Police determined the "victim had lied" in 29 percent of Edmonton unfounded cases, 21 percent of the Hamilton unfounded cases, and 14 percent of the Calgary unfounded cases. This would suggest that false allegations occurred in less than five percent of the total number of cases reported to police in Hamilton and less than two percent of the total number of reports in Calgary.

Clearance Rates

As indicated by Figure 3.4, the clearance rate of cases (i.e., cleared by charge) also varies considerably across the study sites. Note that the highest cleared by charge rate was obtained in Saskatoon, i.e., 46 percent. The lowest cleared by charge rate was found in Edmonton, with 25 percent of their cases being cleared by charge. The rate of clearances by charge from Saskatoon (46 percent) and Calgary (44 percent) compares favourably with the clearance rates for all sexual offences in 1988, when the rate was 46 percent for Alberta, 49 percent for Saskatchewan and 47 percent for Ontario.

Lower than expected clearance rates, however, may be more a function of record-keeping protocol than an indicator of police performance. The findings of the Calgary and Edmonton study are a case in point. In Calgary, cases that are in progress are input on the information system at the investigating officer's discretion. Thus, many investigations may be ongoing that are not being counted as cases "not cleared." In contrast, in Edmonton, when a constable responds to a call for service, the computer system automatically sets up a file number and the investigating constable must input information. Data from the Alberta study seem to support this explanation since 60 percent of Edmonton cases (n=961) were classified as not cleared compared to 34 percent of Calgary cases (n=492). This

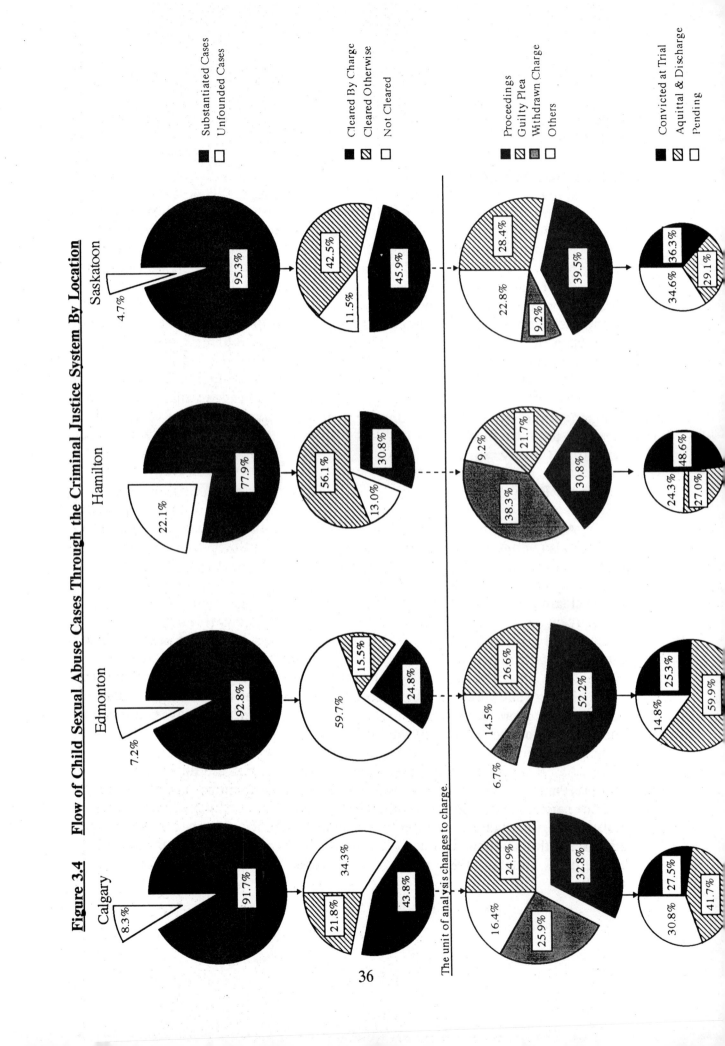

Figure 3.4 Flow of Child Sexual Abuse Cases Through the Criminal Justice System By Location

issue has also recently been raised in a study by the Canadian Centre for Justice Statistics (1990).

## Distribution of Charges

Many of the occurrences of child sexual abuse where charges were laid resulted in multiple charges. For example, in Calgary, 41 percent of the cases involved two charges, and three or more charges were laid in 14 percent of the cases. Multiple charges were also common in Edmonton, where 30 percent of the cases resulted in two charges, and 22 percent resulted in three or more charges. In Saskatchewan, multiple charges occurred less frequently since only 25 percent of the cases resulted in two charges and less than five percent resulted in three or more charges.

As Figure 3.4 indicates, the largest proportion of charges in Calgary (33 percent), Edmonton (52 percent) and Saskatchewan (40 percent) resulted in "not guilty" pleas and proceeded to preliminary inquiry and/or trial (compared to 31 percent of Hamilton cases). The largest relative proportion of Hamilton cases (38 percent) resulted in withdrawn charges. Overall, guilty pleas were very high since a significant percentage of Calgary (25 percent), Edmonton (27 percent), Saskatchewan (28 percent) and Hamilton (22 percent) charges also resulted in guilty pleas. The only unexpected finding was that 26 percent of the charges laid in Calgary and 38 percent of the charges laid in Hamilton were withdrawn. Such high withdrawn rates could be due to the practice of laying multiple charges and then dropping one of the charges to obtain a guilty plea.

## Conviction Rates

Figure 3.4 presents the conviction rates for cases "convicted at trial." These rates range from a low of 25 percent for Edmonton to a high of 49 percent for Hamilton. Conviction rates at trial, however, do not include guilty pleas and thus give only a partial picture of overall conviction consistent with the operational definition presented in Section 2.3.2 of this report. Therefore, analysis of overall conviction rates is presented in Figure 3.5.

As Figure 3.5 indicates, overall conviction rates ranged from a low of 59 percent for Edmonton to a high of 83 percent for Hamilton. All of the study sites' conviction rates compare favourably to rates reported by previous studies. Loh (1980), for example, reported a conviction rate of 57 percent for assault and 59 percent for rape in a United States study. More recently, in a Canadian study, Hann and Kopelman (1987) reported a conviction rate of 73 percent for sexual assaults.

**Figure 3.5**   **Conviction Rates for Child Sexual Abuse By Location**[1]

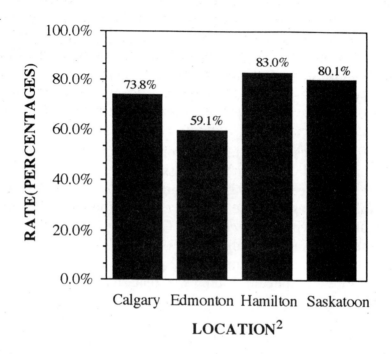

---

[1] Conviction rates based on formula in section 2.3.2 of this report.

[2] Conviction rate is not available for Regina.

The relatively high conviction rate for all sites appears to be due largely to high proportions of guilty pleas. In addition, a significant proportion of Calgary and Hamilton cases involved the withdrawal of charges, which would tend to increase the conviction rate because withdrawn charges do not count against the conviction rate.

An examination of conviction rates by court type provided interesting results. As Figure 3.6 indicates, the highest rate of in court convictions is obtained in Provincial Youth Court under the <u>Young Offenders Act</u>. Of the cases that went to Youth Court in Calgary (conviction rate=96 percent), Edmonton (conviction rate=69 percent) and Saskatchewan (conviction rate=86 percent), the vast majority of young offenders were convicted. Provincial Criminal Court conviction rates of adult accused were significantly less with 50 percent for Calgary cases and 61 percent for Edmonton cases. There were too few Saskatchewan cases to make a reliable comparison.

Cases of adult accused tried in Queen's Bench Court (judges appointed by federal government) were also significantly less likely to result in a conviction. Note that the highest conviction rate for this court was obtained in Edmonton (i.e., 36 percent compared to 35 percent for Calgary and only 28 percent for Saskatchewan).

<u>Rates of Incarceration</u>

Previous studies have found that for sexual assault incarceration rates range from 55 percent (EKOS Research Associates, 1988) to 66 percent (Roberts 1990a). As Figure 3.7 demonstrates, the site study findings on incarceration compare favourably with previous studies. The lowest rate of incarceration was 51 percent for Edmonton convictions. The highest rate of incarceration was 74 percent for convictions in Hamilton.

## 3.5 Decision Making in the Criminal Justice System

This section of the report identifies the factors which are associated with the decision to lay charges by the various police departments included in the site studies. In order to facilitate the identification of the factors which predict investigations resulting in charges being laid, the Knowledge Seeker program was employed. This multivariate program was used to identify the best predictors of cleared by charge status from the list of predictors (i.e., independent variables) (see Appendix B Tables). The data for each of the sites were analyzed separately.

**Figure 3.6   Conviction Rates for Child Sexual Abuse By Court Type and Location[1]**

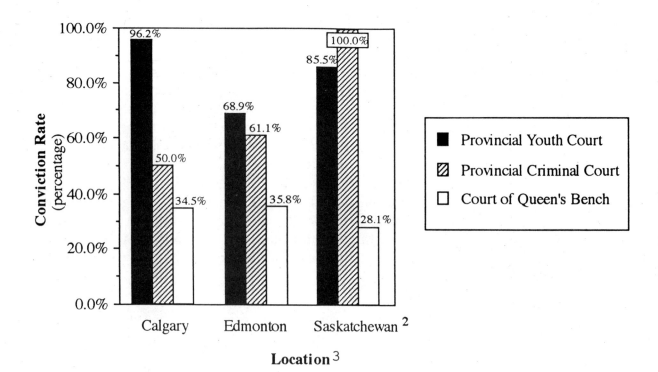

[1] These conviction rates are based on the ratio of conviction acquittal on completion of court proceedings. Guilty pleas within proceedings are not used in the calculation.

[2] The 100.0% conviction rate for Saskatchewan Provincial Court must be interpreted with caution since it involves only three cases.

[3] Data for conviction rates by court type are not available for Hamilton.

**Figure 3.7    Incarceration Rates for Child Sexual Abuse By Location**

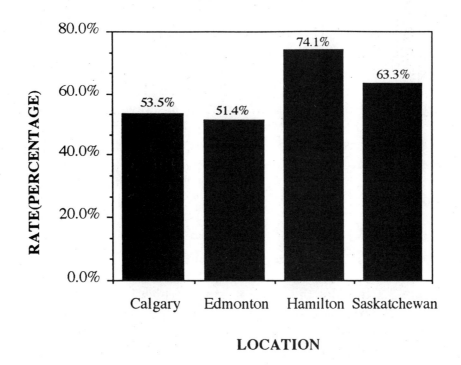

However, for the sake of comparison, the first two iterations, or levels of the stepwise function, are contained in Figure 3.8 for all locations.[5]

### 3.5.1 Decision to Lay Charges: Calgary

Figure 3.8 contains the decision model "tree" which best predicts whether cases are cleared by charge, as opposed to those cleared otherwise and not cleared, for Calgary cases. The best predictor of cleared by charge is the presence of witnesses in the case (i.e., 82 percent compared to 57 percent for no witnesses). For cases having witnesses, the second iteration shows that lengthy abuse, from 91 days to more than one year, raises the probability of being charged to 92 percent.

Figure 3.8 also shows that in cases having no witnesses, age of the victim is positively correlated to being charged up to the age of 14 years old. Note, for example, that in cases involving no witnesses, charges were laid in less than 21 percent of the cases involving child victims under four years of age, compared to 52 percent for victims five to 11 years old and 81 percent for victims 12 and 13 years old.

### 3.5.2 Decision to Lay Charges: Edmonton

Figure 3.8 contains the decision model which best predicts whether Edmonton cases are cleared by charge, as opposed to cleared otherwise and not cleared. The first variable to split (and thus the best predictor from the list of independent variables shown in Table 3.5 to predict cleared by charge) is "when the occurrence was reported." Note that when the alleged incident was reported immediately, 91 percent of the cases were concluded by laying charges compared to only 32 percent of the cases when no date was recorded (i.e., no specific disclosure occurred). In the second iteration, the number of victims became the most significant predictor. Cases involving more than one victim were cleared by charge 93 percent of the time, compared to 75 percent of the cases involving only one victim.

---

[5] More detailed analysis of the decision making process is presented in the individual site reports.

### 3.5.3 Decision to Lay Charges: Hamilton

The results in Figure 3.8 indicated that in Hamilton the decision to charge is strongly influenced by the age of the victim. Note that there was a higher rate of charging among cases in both of the older age categories than among those where the victim was under eight years old. For the youngest children, however, the presence of a witness was very important in the decision to charge (50 percent of the cases having witnesses were cleared by charge, compared to eight percent where no witnesses were present). It is interesting to note that the gender of the victim is related to charging in the case of 12 and 13 year olds. An unanticipated finding, though, is that for cases involving 12 and 13 year old victims, there is a greater likelihood that offences involving male victims resulted in charges. Given the relatively small number of cases in this category (n=15), however, it would not be appropriate to generalize from this finding.

### 3.5.4 Decision to Lay Charges: Saskatchewan

Figure 3.8 also contains the decision model for cases charged versus those cleared otherwise for Saskatchewan. Age of the accused was the best predictor of whether or not a charge is laid. Note that 73 percent of accused in the age categories 16 to 25 years and 36 years and older were charged, while 63 percent of accused 26 to 35 years of age were charged and only 50 percent of accused 12 to 15 years of age were charged. For those accused in the 12 to 15 year age category, duration of abuse also contributed to charges being laid. The greatest number of charges were laid in those cases for which the abuse was ongoing for more than one year (82 percent). Those cases for which there was just one occurrence to less than one year obtained a lower probability (52 percent) of being charged.

For those accused in the 16 to 25 year and over 35 year categories, the time lapsed between the last incident and the report to the police was also a significant predictor of being charged. The greatest number of accused in this age group were charged when the report occurred within the period, one day to one year (81 percent), followed closely by those cases in which the report occurred either within the first 24 hours or after one year (71 percent). Those cases for which no date was recorded (i.e., there was no clear disclosure) had the lowest charge rate for these age groups (27 percent).

**Figure 3.8    Decision Model for Cleared By Charge Cases of Child Sexual Abuse By Location**

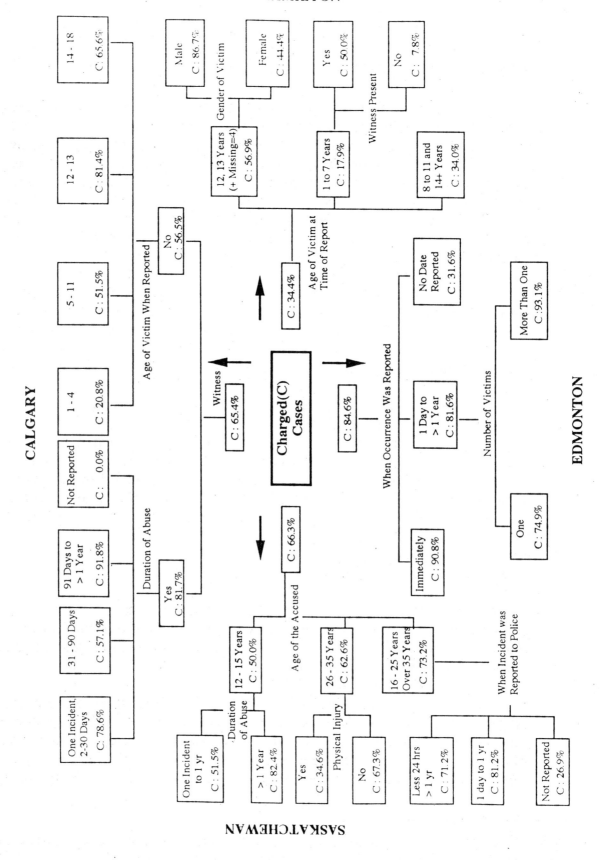

### 3.5.5 Trends in the Decision to Lay Charges

An overview of the findings regarding the decision to lay charges reveals some relatively similar trends. First, age of the victim emerged as an important predictor of laying charges for both the Calgary and Hamilton cases. The age of the victim in both locations was positively associated with charges being laid, except that the positive effect of age diminished in both Calgary and Hamilton for those 14 years and over. This finding would suggest that, as the alleged victim approaches the age when dating and sexual activity became acceptable, they are more likely to become involved in situations where the consent of the alleged victim becomes an issue.

Another variable that was significant for both the Hamilton and Calgary cases was whether witnesses, usually corroborative, were involved in the case. If they were present, it significantly increased the probability that the investigation would conclude with charges being laid. The importance of a witness in Calgary and Hamilton, as well as the importance of more than one victim in Edmonton, would seem to suggest the importance of corroboration to the police in laying charges.

The duration of the abuse was also identified as a significant predictor of charges being laid in two of the sites, Calgary and Saskatchewan. In both locations, longer duration was associated with laying charges. The exception to this trend was the finding for Edmonton that cases involving isolated occurrences reported immediately had the highest probability of being cleared by charge.

## 3.6 Case Duration

Table 3.3 presents data on the average duration of cases from the time of first occurrence through various stages to conclusion of the trial for Calgary, Edmonton and Hamilton cases.[6] Saskatchewan data were not comparable and thus are not referred to in this section.

The average time duration from the first occurrence to report to police ranged from a low of five months for Hamilton cases to a high of 21 months for Calgary cases. However, high standard deviations of 929 days for Calgary and 445 days for Hamilton cases indicate a broad range of duration of over a year or more. Next, the elapsed time between report to police and preliminary inquiry

---

[6] While "average" times are discussed in this section, please note that the standard deviation is very high in most categories, indicating extreme variation.

## Table 3.3   Average Elapsed Time Between First Occurrence, Most Recent Occurrence, Report to Police, Preliminary Inquiry and Trial, By Location[1]

| Time Period | Calgary | | | Edmonton | | | Hamilton | | |
|---|---|---|---|---|---|---|---|---|---|
| | n | s.d. | $\bar{X}$ days (months) | n | s.d. | $\bar{X}$ days (months) | n | s.d. | $\bar{X}$ days (months) |
| First Occurrence to Report to Police | 313 | 929.4 | 627.4 (20.9) | 460 | 808.8 | 374.8 (12.5) | 210 | 445.0 | 149.0 (5.0) |
| Most Recent Occurrence to Report to Police | 300 | 547.7 | 243.6 (8.1) | 456 | 460.6 | 152.6 (5.1) | 245 | 328.2 | 80.3 (2.7) |
| Report to Police to Preliminary Inquiry | 99 | 125.4 | 159.3 (5.3) | 140 | 82.5 | 155.3 (5.2) | 37 | 66.6 | 270.8 (9.0) |
| Report to Police to Trial | 220 | 173.6 | 268.8 (9.0) | 331 | 164.4 | 245.0 (8.2) | 33 | 109.7 | 320.5 (10.7) |
| Preliminary Inquiry to Trial | 100 | 107.4 | 195.0 (6.5) | 139 | 113.0 | 207.0 (6.9) | 19 | 87.1 | 69.7 (2.3) |
| First Occurrence to Trial | 218 | 986.2 | 927.0 (30.9) | 331 | 930.2 | 629.1 (21.0) | 17 | 568.9 | 691.7 (23.1) |
| Most Recent Occurrence to Trial | 207 | 612.9 | 518.4 (17.3) | 327 | 573.9 | 440.3 (14.7) | 26 | 323.3 | 417.6 (13.9) |

---

[1] Case duration data from Saskatchewan are not comparable.

was consistent for Calgary (5.3 months) and Edmonton (5.2 months), but significantly longer (i.e., 9 months) for Hamilton cases. In contrast, Hamilton cases proceeded more quickly from preliminary inquiry to trial (i.e., 2.3 months) than Calgary (6.5 months), or Edmonton (6.9 months). The overall time duration from report to police to trial ranged from a low of eight months for Edmonton cases to a high of 11 months for Hamilton cases.

## 3.7 Child Victim/Witnesses in the Court Process

Because of the small number of child victim/witnesses observed in court proceedings in Hamilton (12 observations) and Saskatchewan (21 observations), data analysis for these locations was limited, for the most part, to qualitative analysis. In Calgary and Edmonton, however, a sufficient number of cases were observed and the results of a multivariate Knowledge Seeker analysis are presented below. Analysis was conducted using 30 independent variables run on three dependent variables: anxious/withdrawn; sad/cries; and ability to communicate (see Appendix B, Table B-4). Findings will be presented for each location because the victim/witnesses observed in Edmonton were significantly older than those observed in Calgary.

### 3.7.1 Overall Impression

Before focussing on the Edmonton and Calgary cases, it is interesting to note the consistency of the impressions of the researchers who observed the children in court. The Saskatchewan study concluded:

> Court observation data showed that overall, child witnesses exhibited a relatively positive response to the experience of testifying in court, suggesting that they were coping reasonably well under very difficult circumstances. Analysis of child witnesses' ability to communicate showed that ability to communicate was lowest during the oath/communication stage, highest during examination-in-chief and intermediate during the cross-examination. (Fischer et al., 1992)

Likewise, the Hamilton researchers concluded the following:

> From the court observation material, the overall impression is that the children were in fact very competent witnesses. The judge asked the child to speak louder on only four occasions. The principal questioner (at any given point) asked the child to speak louder or give a verbal response from one to four times in one-third of the

observations (i.e., 12 of 34 points at which the rating was carried out for the 11 children). The judge questioned a child on one-third (i.e., 11) of the rating occasions, with the number of questions ranging from one (in 4 cases) to 12 (in one case). The purpose of the judge's questions was primarily to expand or clarify factual information being given by the child (8 of 11). This was followed in importance by questions aimed at assessing the child's competence (4 of 11). (Campbell et al., 1992)

3.7.2 Child Victim/Witnesses in Court: Calgary

Background Information

Fifteen male victim/witnesses (21 percent) and 58 female victim/witnesses (80 percent) were observed in court in Calgary from August 1, 1989 to July 31, 1990. Their ages ranged from six years old (n=7, ten percent) to 18 years old. However, the majority of children (58 percent) were between 12 and 15 years old.

The most frequently experienced levels of intrusion were genital fondling (18 percent), vaginal penetration with penis (18 percent), oral sex (14 percent), and digital penetration (14 percent). Most of the observations were either in a Queen's Bench preliminary inquiry held in Provincial Court (51 percent), or at a Queen's Bench trial (47 percent). Only two youth court proceedings were observed.

Anxious/Withdrawn

The most significant predictor of the child being highly anxious/withdrawn in the court process was physical injuries. The children who had experienced physical injury during the abuse incident(s) demonstrated significantly higher anxiety (82 percent) than those children who had not been physcially injured (48 percent). The second most important variable for those children who did not experience physical injury was the presence of expert witnesses. This could indicate that these children, while not suffering physical injury, might have experienced a higher proportion of emotional injury and/or been involved in more complex cases, thus requiring the presence of expert witnesses (see Appendix B, Figure B-1).

### Sad/Cries

No variables were significantly correlated to the sad/cries subscale in the Calgary sample.

### Ability to Communicate

Only one variable (when occurrence was reported to police) obtained a significant relationship to the dependent variable ability to communicate. Note that incidents reported "immediately" had a high correlation with ability to communicate. In contrast, when the abuse was reported more than one year after it occurred, or if it was vague and no date was recorded, then only 13 percent demonstrated a high ability to communicate (see Appendix B, Figure B-2).

## 3.7.3 Child Victim/Witnesses in Court: Edmonton

### Background Information

Seventeen male victim/witnesses (32 percent) and 37 female victim/witnesses (69 percent) were observed in court in Edmonton from August 1, 1989 to July 31, 1990. Their ages ranged from seven years old to 18 years old; 44 percent were 16 to 18 years old, 44 percent were between 12 and 15 years old. There were five children between eight and 11 years old and one seven year old. The most frequently experienced level of intrusion was genital fondling (45 percent), followed by vaginal penetration (27 percent) and mutual genital fondling (eight percent).

Most observations were made in a Queen's Bench preliminary inquiry held in Provincial Court (45 percent), and a Queen's Bench trial (46 percent); however, four observations were also made in Provincial Criminal Court and one was made in youth court.

### Anxious/Withdrawn

The first and only variable to emerge in predicting anxious/withdrawn behaviour was the number of court appearances. Child witnesses who had experienced two or more court appearances were high on the anxious/withdrawn subscale compared to children who were in court for the first time or who only had one previous experience. One obvious explanation for this finding is that "having to tell the story repeatedly" and being challenged results in stress (see Appendix B, Figure B-3).

### Sad/Cries

Again, as with anxious/withdrawn above, the number of previous court appearances is the most significant predictor of the sad/cries subscale. Obviously, children who had to retell their stories found it difficult. A second iteration indicates that witnesses being cleared from the courtroom during the testimony is an important predictor of the sad/cries subscale for those children who have only been in court once or never before. Note, for example, when witnesses are not cleared, both of the child victim witnesses (100 percent) obtained high scores on the sad/cries subscale compared to 18 percent of the cases where witnesses were cleared. Further, the information indicates a tendency for the female victim/witnesses to score higher on the sad/cries subscale (see Appendix B, Figure B-4).

### Ability to Communicate

The first and only variable in predicting ability to communicate was the number of people in the courtroom. When there were less than ten people in the courtroom, 79 percent of the witnesses demonstrated high ability to communicate, compared to 53 percent for situations where more than ten people were in the courtroom (see Appendix B, Figure B-5).

## 3.8 Summary

### 3.8.1 The Interrelationship Between the Child Welfare System and Criminal Justice System

### Protocols

- There was a high degree of inter-agency cooperation in the development of protocols for dealing with child sexual abuse both in Ontario and Alberta.

- In Ontario, the Catholic Children's Aid Society tended to investigate all allegations of child sexual abuse (i.e., both intra and extrafamilial). The Children's Aid Society, however, tended to investigate only intrafamilial cases of child sexual abuse.

- In Alberta, child welfare authorities tended to investigate intrafamilial child sexual abuse cases (i.e., where the child was considered to be in need of protection) because the perpetrator and the victim lived in the same household.

## Special Police Units

- Calgary and Edmonton, Alberta, and Hamilton, Ontario police all had special child abuse investigation units.

## Overlap of Cases

- Almost all of the Hamilton, Ontario child sexual abuse cases were formally investigated (i.e., were "active" files) by both child welfare and police agencies, compared to less than one-half of the Calgary and Edmonton, Alberta cases.

- In Alberta, cases which did not have an active child welfare file tended to involve accused who were strangers to the child (i.e., extrafamilial cases). This finding is consistent with the application of the "principle of least intrusion" expressed by Alberta child welfare legislation.

### 3.8.2 The Processing of Cases in the Criminal Justice System

## Reporting Rates

- Reporting of alleged occurrences of child sexual abuse was high in all jurisdictions, ranging from a low of 73 per 100,000 in 1990 for Hamilton to a high of 158 per 100,000 in 1989 in Saskatoon.

- Children are significantly over represented as victims of sexual assault.

## Case Profiles

- Profiles of victims, accused, and occurrences were very similar across all study sites.

- Most victims were female under 12 years old and a significant number were under five years old (15 to 22 percent).

- The majority of accused (94 percent) were male, often related to the victim (30 to 57 percent).

- A significant number (17 to 29 percent) of the accused were 12 to 17 years old, and therefore were charged under the Young Offenders Act.

- The most common form of abuse was genital fondling. Intercourse occurred in ten to 20 percent of the cases.

## Unfounded Rates

- Unfounded rates were generally low, ranging from a low of five percent in Saskatoon to a high of 22 percent in Hamilton.

- False allegations of abuse (victim lied) occurred in only two to five percent of the total reports.

## Clearance Rates

- There was considerable variation in clearance rates (i.e., cleared by charge) across study sites, due mainly to record-keeping protocols of the various police agencies.

## Conviction Rates

- Conviction rates for all child sexual assaults were generally high, ranging from a low of 59 percent in Edmonton to a high of 83 percent in Hamilton.

- Youth court (under the Young Offenders Act) obtained a significantly higher conviction rate than provincial or federal adult court.

## Incarceration Rates

- Incarceration rates ranged from a low of 51 percent in Edmonton to a high of 74 percent in Hamilton.

## Case Duration

- Average case duration (i.e., from report to police to trial) ranged from a low of eight months in Edmonton to a high of 11 months in Hamilton.

## Child Performance in Court

- Children who were physically harmed during the incident had more difficulty presenting evidence than those who were not physically injured.

- Children had difficulty "telling the story" if a long period of time had passed since the incident.

- Fewer strangers in the courtroom and more supportive adults made it easier for the child to give evidence.

- Cross-examination by defence lawyers was significantly the most stressful part of the court process for the child victim/witness.

# 4.0 IMPLEMENTATION AND IMPACT OF BILL C-15, <u>AN ACT TO AMEND THE CRIMINAL CODE AND THE CANADA EVIDENCE ACT</u>

This chapter focusses specifically on the implementation and impact of Bill C-15, and is most relevant to the third major purpose of the site studies:

(3) to identify the degree to which the goals and objectives of Bill C-15, <u>An Act to Amend the Criminal Code and the Canada Evidence Act</u>, have been achieved.

The analysis of data in this chapter will be structured according to the specific goals and related objectives of Bill C-15 discussed in Chapter 1.0, Section 1.3.

## 4.1 Goal # 1: To Provide Better Protection to Child Sexual Abuse Victim/Witnesses

The findings relevant to Goal # 1 of Bill C-15 are presented below as they relate to the four specific objectives or expected outcomes.

### 4.1.1 Objective # 1: To Broaden the Range of Conduct Captured by the Criminal Code

As discussed in Chapter 1.0, one intended outcome of Bill C-15 was to increase the range of conduct captured by the <u>Criminal Code</u>. The specific amendments that are related to this objective are the repeal of subsection 146(1) XCC (Intercourse with a female under 14 years) and subsection 146(2) XCC (Intercourse with a female 14 to 16 years). These sections were replaced by section 151 CC (Sexual interference), section 152 CC (Invitation to sexual touching), and section 153 CC (Sexual exploitation).

Sexual interference was designed to increase the protection for girls and boys against a wide range of sexual acts not covered under the old law. Section 152 makes it an offence for a person to invite or encourage a child under the age of 14 years to touch him/her or any other person for sexual gratification. Section 153 extends protection to boys and girls between 14 and 17 years from sexual exploitation (broadened from sexual intercourse) by someone in a position of trust or authority over them. In order to reflect on the extent to which this objective has been accomplished, the number of charges, associated behaviours and conviction rates for sections 151, 152, and 153 were examined for the study locations.

### Number of Charges for Sections 151 (Sexual Interference), 152 (Invitation to Sexual Touching), 153 (Sexual Exploitation)

Figure 4.1 indicates a trend toward overall increase in the total number of sexual assault related charges for Calgary, Edmonton and Saskatchewan. In Calgary, the 1988 increase over 1987 was over 20 percent, followed by a further increase of 22 percent in 1989, and then a slight decrease of less than 12 percent in 1990. Overall in Calgary, from 1987 to 1990, the number of charges laid increased by 30 percent.

Calgary

To a large extent, these overall increases in Calgary are a function of the increases in charges under sections 151, 152 and 153 compared to the old subsections 146(1) and (2). There were only five charges laid under section 146 in 1986 and six in 1987. In comparison, 61 charges were laid under the new codes in 1988, 102 in 1989 and 105 in 1990. Most of the charges were laid under section 151, while section 153 has been the least used section (i.e., two charges in 1988, eight in 1989 and six in 1990). As a group, however, it is clear that the new codes (i.e., sections 151, 152, 153) were employed significantly more frequently than the old codes (i.e., subsections 146(1) and (2)), particularly in 1989 and 1990. There has also been a significant corresponding increase in the number of charges laid under section 271 (Sexual assault), however, the relative proportion of charges laid under section 271 continued to decrease (i.e., in 1990 it accounted for 47 percent of the charges).

Edmonton

The pattern of charges under sections relevant to child sexual abuse and assault in Edmonton, from 1986 to 1990, was similar to Calgary. An overall increase in the total number of relevant charges is apparent. In 1988 the increase over 1987 was 19 percent, followed by a further increase of six percent in 1989 and 27 percent in 1990. Overall, the number of charges laid increased by 60 percent from 1987 to 1990.

Most of the overall increases were due to the increase in the number of charges under sections 151, 152 and 153 compared to the old subsections 146(1) and (2). For example, only 15 charges were laid under subsection 146(1) in 1986, and eight in 1987. In comparison, 32 charges were laid under the new codes sections 151, 152 and 153 in 1988, 62 in 1989 and 95 in 1990. Most of the charges

**Figure 4.1** **Number of Charges under Specific Sections Relevant to Child Sexual Abuse in Calgary, Edmonton, and Saskatchewan from 1986 to 1990[1]**

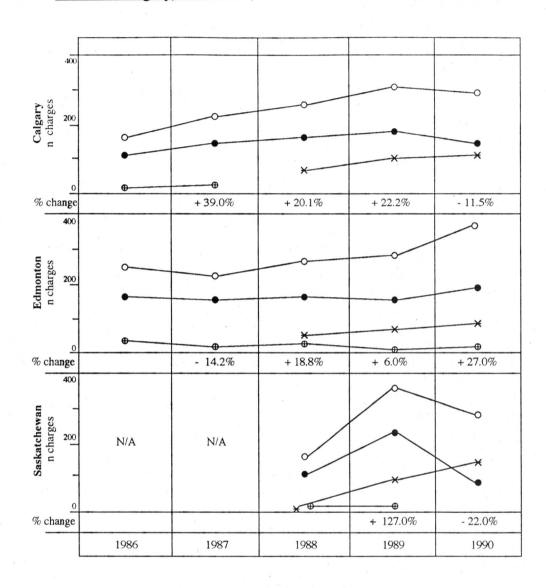

Key:  ⊕  ss 146(1) and (2)
● ss 246.1, 246.2, 246.3, s.271
✕ ss 151, 152, 153
○ All charges relevant to child sexual assault

---

[1] Comparable data are not available for Hamilton. However, for 1990, total number of child sexual assault charges = 120 (s. 271 = 53(44.2%)); ss. 151 and 152 = 35(29.2%)). See Appendix B, Tables B-5, B-6 and B-7 for the frequency of specific charges.

were laid under section 151 and the fewest were laid under section 153. As a group, however, it is clear that the new codes were employed significantly more frequently than the old codes, particularly in 1989 and 1990. The number of charges under section 271 was relatively stable up to 1990, when there was a significant increase in the number of charges (i.e., n=191), while the relative proportion of charges laid under this section continued to decrease (i.e., in 1990 it accounted for 53 percent of the total charges).

Saskatchewan

Data on charges related to child sexual assault were also available from the Saskatchewan study for the years 1988 to 1990. As Figure 4.1 indicates, there was an overall increase of 76 percent in the total number of charges from 1988 to 1990. This included a 127 percent increase during the year 1989, followed by a decrease of 22 percent during 1990. The number of charges under the newly created sections 151, 152 and 153 increased, while those under the old subsections 146(1) and (2), as well as under section 271, decreased significantly.

Hamilton

In Hamilton in 1990, 120 charges related to child sexual assault were laid. While trend data were not available, it is interesting to note that over 44 percent of these charges were made under section 271 and over 29 percent were made under sections 151 and 152. In comparison, 38 percent of the 1990 charges in Calgary were under sections 151, 152 and 153, while the proportions for Edmonton and Saskatchewan were 27 percent and 54 percent respectively.

Overall Trends

Overall, the findings indicate: (a) an increased application of all sexual assault legislation over time; (b) the continued use of the more general assault legislation, i.e., section 271 -- except for Saskatchewan; and (c) adoption and use of section 151.

## Behaviours Associated with Sections 151 (Sexual Interference), 152 (Invitation to Sexual Touching) and 153 (Sexual Exploitation)

Section 151 (Sexual Interference)

Table 4.1 contains a breakdown of the types of behaviour that occurred in cases where charges were laid under sections 151, 152 and 153, as well as subsection 173(2) (Exposure to child under 14 years).

Table 4.1 Range of Conduct for Cases Having Charges Under Sections 151, 152, 153 or 173(2) of the New Criminal Code, By Location[1]

| Location and Section | | Exposure | Invitation | Show Porno-graphy | Undress | Masturba-tion | Inappro-priate Kissing | Chest Fondling | Buttocks Fondling | Genital Fondling | Victim Fondled Offender |
|---|---|---|---|---|---|---|---|---|---|---|---|
| **NUMBER OF CASES INVOLVING** | | | | | | | | | | | |
| **Calgary** | | | | | | | | | | | |
| s.151 | n | 21 | 7 | 7 | 28 | 13 | 31 | 48 | 11 | 97 | 31 |
|  | % | 14.9 | 5.0 | 5.0 | 19.9 | 9.2 | 22.0 | 34.0 | 7.8 | 68.8 | 22.0 |
| s.152 | n | 5 | 2 | 1 | 1 | 2 | 2 | 3 | - | 4 | 7 |
|  | % | 50.0 | 20.0 | 10.0 | 10.0 | 20.0 | 20.0 | 30.0 | - | 40.0 | 70.0 |
| s.153 | n | 5 | - | 3 | 5 | 4 | 5 | 10 | 3 | 12 | 4 |
|  | % | 26.3 | - | 15.8 | 26.3 | 21.1 | 26.3 | 52.6 | 15.8 | 63.2 | 21.1 |
| s.173(2)[2] | n | - | - | - | - | - | - | - | - | - | - |
|  | % | - | - | - | - | - | - | - | - | - | - |
| **Edmonton** | | | | | | | | | | | |
| s.151 | n | 6 | 8 | 3 | 3 | 7 | 13 | 24 | 16 | 50 | 15 |
|  | % | 8.3 | 11.1 | 4.2 | 4.2 | 9.7 | 18.1 | 33.3 | 22.2 | 69.4 | 20.8 |
| s.152 | n | 8 | 10 | 3 | 4 | 5 | 1 | 2 | 2 | 8 | 8 |
|  | % | 40.0 | 50.0 | 15.0 | 20.0 | 25.0 | 5.0 | 10.0 | 10.0 | 40.0 | 40.0 |
| s.153 | n | 1 | - | 1 | 2 | - | 1 | 5 | - | 6 | 1 |
|  | % | 14.3 | - | 14.3 | 28.6 | - | 14.3 | 71.4 | - | 85.7 | 14.3 |
| s.173(2)[2] | n | 22 | - | - | - | - | - | - | - | - | - |
|  | % | 100.0 | - | - | - | - | - | - | - | - | - |
| **Hamilton** | | | | | | | | | | | |
| s.151 | n | 3 | 3 | - | 3 | - | 4 | 8 | 2 | 14 | 10 |
|  | % | 10.0 | 10.0 | - | 10.0 | - | 13.3 | 26.7 | 6.7 | 46.7 | 33.3 |
| s.152 | n | 1 | 3 | - | - | - | - | 1 | - | 2 | - |
|  | % | 25.0 | 75.0 | - | - | - | - | 25.0 | - | 50.0 | - |
| s.153 | n | - | 1 | - | 1 | - | 1 | 2 | - | 8 | 2 |
|  | % | - | 11.1 | - | 11.1 | - | 11.1 | 22.2 | - | 88.9 | 22.2 |
| s.173(2)[2] | n | 7 | 1 | - | - | - | - | - | - | - | 1 |
|  | % | 100.0 | 14.3 | - | - | - | - | - | - | - | 14.3 |
| **Saskatchewan** | | | | | | | | | | | |
| s.151 | n | 8 | 5 | 2 | 10 | 6 | 17 | 44 | 34 | 110 | 27 |
|  | % | 4.3 | 2.7 | 1.1 | 5.3 | 3.2 | 9.1 | 24.0 | 18.0 | 59.0 | 14.0 |
| s.152 | n | 3 | 6 | - | - | 1 | 3 | 1 | - | 8 | 8 |
|  | % | 17.0 | 33.0 | - | - | 5.6 | 17.0 | 5.6 | - | 44.0 | 44.0 |
| s.153 | n | 2 | 1 | 1 | - | - | 1 | 4 | 2 | 6 | 3 |
|  | % | 13.6 | 6.7 | 5.6 | - | - | 6.7 | 27.0 | 13.0 | 40.0 | 20.0 |
| s.173(2)[2] | n | 2 | 2 | 1 | - | 4 | - | 1 | - | 2 | 1 |
|  | % | 25.0 | 25.0 | 13.0 | - | 50.0 | - | 13.0 | - | 25.0 | 13.0 |

continued .../

Table 4.1    (continued)

| Location and Section | | Forced Activity w/Others | Simulated Intercourse | Vaginal Penetration with Finger | Attempted Vaginal Penetration | Anal Penetration with Finger | Oral Sex on Offender | Oral Sex on Victim | Vaginal Penetration with Penis | Anal Penetration with Penis | Forced Prostitution | Total Cases (n=) |
|---|---|---|---|---|---|---|---|---|---|---|---|---|
| **Calgary** | | | | | | | | | | | | |
| s.151 | n | 2 | 24 | 33 | 5 | 4 | 11 | 26 | 19 | 6 | - | 141 |
|  | % | 1.4 | 17.0 | 23.4 | 3.5 | 2.8 | 7.8 | 18.4 | 13.5 | 4.3 | - | |
| s.152 | n | - | 1 | 3 | - | - | 1 | 4 | 2 | - | - | 10 |
|  | % | - | 10.0 | 30.0 | - | - | 10.0 | 40.0 | 20.0 | - | - | |
| s.153 | n | - | 5 | 2 | 1 | 1 | 3 | 5 | 6 | 1 | - | 19 |
|  | % | - | 26.3 | 10.5 | 5.3 | 5.3 | 15.8 | 26.3 | 31.6 | 5.3 | - | |
| s.173(2)[2] | n | - | - | - | - | - | - | - | - | - | - | 0 |
|  | % | - | - | - | - | - | - | - | - | - | - | |
| **Edmonton** | | | | | | | | | | | | |
| s.151 | n | 3 | 11 | 13 | 4 | 1 | 6 | 9 | 8 | 2 | - | 72 |
|  | % | 4.2 | 15.3 | 18.1 | 5.6 | 1.4 | 8.3 | 12.5 | 11.1 | 2.8 | - | |
| s.152 | n | 5 | - | 2 | 1 | 1 | 3 | 2 | - | 2 | - | 20 |
|  | % | 25.0 | - | 10.0 | 5.0 | 5.0 | 15.0 | 10.0 | - | 10.0 | - | |
| s.153 | n | 1 | - | 2 | - | - | - | 1 | - | - | - | 7 |
|  | % | 14.3 | - | 28.6 | - | - | - | 14.3 | - | - | - | |
| s.173(2)[2] | n | - | - | - | 1 | - | - | - | - | - | - | 22 |
|  | % | - | - | - | 4.5 | - | - | - | - | - | - | |
| **Hamilton** | | | | | | | | | | | | |
| s.151 | n | - | 5 | 4 | - | - | 1 | 5 | 4 | 2 | - | 30 |
|  | % | - | 16.7 | 13.3 | - | - | 3.3 | 16.7 | 13.3 | 6.7 | - | |
| s.152 | n | - | - | - | - | - | 1 | 1 | - | 1 | - | 4 |
|  | % | - | - | - | - | - | 25.0 | 25.0 | - | 25.0 | - | |
| s.153 | n | - | 1 | - | - | - | - | - | 1 | - | - | 9 |
|  | % | - | 11.1 | - | - | - | - | - | 11.1 | - | - | |
| s.173(2)[2] | n | - | - | - | - | - | - | - | 1 | - | - | 7 |
|  | % | - | - | - | - | - | - | - | 14.3 | - | - | |
| **Saskatchewan** | | | | | | | | | | | | |
| s.151 | n | 4 | 26 | 25 | 18 | 4 | 29 | 21 | 27 | 5 | - | 187 |
|  | % | 2.1 | 14.0 | 13.0 | 9.6 | 2.1 | 16.0 | 11.0 | 14.0 | 2.7 | - | |
| s.152 | n | 2 | 2 | 1 | 1 | - | 5 | 1 | - | 1 | - | 18 |
|  | % | 11.0 | 11.0 | 5.6 | 5.6 | - | 28.0 | 5.6 | - | 5.6 | - | |
| s.153 | n | 2 | 3 | 1 | 1 | 1 | 3 | 3 | 2 | - | - | 15 |
|  | % | 13.0 | 20.0 | 6.7 | 6.7 | 6.7 | 20.0 | 20.0 | 13.0 | - | - | |
| s.173(2)[2] | n | - | 1 | 1 | 1 | - | 1 | 1 | - | - | - | 8 |
|  | % | - | 13.0 | 13.0 | 13.0 | - | 13.0 | 13.0 | - | - | - | |

Data Sources: Police File Review; Unit of Analysis: Case (victim/occurrence)

[1] Throughout this table, "Total Cases" refers to all cases having at least one charge under the specified section. Note that other charges may also be present, and will therefore contribute to the behaviour present.

[2] For section 173(2), cases are only included in this table if the child was under 14 years of age when abuse began. For the remaining sections, all cases are included, regardless of age.

Under section 151, note that the most frequently reported activity was genital fondling in all four locations. The highest frequency of genital fondling recorded was 69 percent for Edmonton and Calgary cases charged under section 151, and the lowest was 47 percent for Hamilton. The rate for Saskatchewan cases was 59 percent. The second and third most frequently reported behaviours involved either chest fondling, buttock fondling or, in the case of Hamilton occurrences, the victim fondling the offender (33 percent). Only a few of the cases charged under section 151 involved vaginal penetration with penis -- Calgary, Hamilton and Saskatchewan cases, for example, all obtained approximately 14 percent, while Edmonton rated slightly lower with 11 percent.

Section 152 (Invitation to Sexual Touching)

In comparison with section 151, there were significantly fewer cases involving charges laid under section 152 in all locations. For these cases, however, the pattern of behaviour reported was as broad as that associated with section 151 discussed above, but somewhat different. First, victim fondling the offender was common for Calgary (70 percent), Edmonton (40 percent) and Saskatchewan cases (44 percent), but was not reported in any of the four Hamilton cases. Exposure was also frequently reported in cases at all sites (i.e., ranging from 50 percent for Calgary cases to 17 percent for Saskatchewan cases). Finally, invitation was reported for 75 percent of the Hamilton cases, 50 percent of the Edmonton cases, 33 percent of the Saskatchewan cases, and 20 percent of the Calgary cases. Intercourse was reported in only two cases in Calgary.

Section 153 (Sexual Exploitation)

The behaviour pattern associated with section 153 was very similar to that associated with section 151. Specifically, genital fondling was again reported most frequently by all sites -- i.e., 89 percent for Hamilton, 86 percent for Edmonton, 63 percent for Calgary and 40 percent for Saskatchewan cases. Chest fondling was also reported in a significant number of cases in Calgary (53 percent) and Edmonton (71 percent). Vaginal penetration with the penis occurred in 32 percent of the Calgary cases, but was not frequently reported for other locations. In conclusion, it is obvious from the data that, in all locations, the new sections 151, 152 and 153 are covering a significantly broad range of conduct, not just intercourse.

Conviction Rates

Section 151 (Sexual Interference)

As Figure 4.2 indicates, the overall conviction rates for charges laid under section 151 varied from a high of 89 percent for Saskatchewan cases to a low of 52 percent for Calgary cases. Edmonton and Hamilton cases obtained conviction rates of 62 percent and 80 percent respectively. These relatively high conviction rates are due to high rates of guilty pleas, particularly in Edmonton (19 percent) and Saskatchewan (15 percent), and high rates of charges withdrawn in Hamilton (50 percent) and Calgary (38 percent).

Section 152 (Invitation to Sexual Touching)

Because of the small number of cases charged under section 152 in all locations (i.e., Calgary=10; Edmonton=20; Hamilton=4; and Saskatchewan=18), a detailed analysis is not warranted. However, based on the data available, the rates of conviction are high in all locations, ranging from a high of 100 percent in Calgary and Hamilton to a low of 63 percent for Saskatchewan cases. The conviction rate for Edmonton was 85 percent.

Section 153 (Sexual Exploitation)

There were even fewer charges laid under section 153 than under section 152. Calgary police used this section the most, laying 19 charges in almost three years, none of which resulted in a conviction or a guilty plea. Hamilton police laid 13 charges under this section in one year, but nine were withdrawn and four were stayed. Edmonton had seven charges laid, resulting in a 50 percent conviction rate, and Saskatchewan police laid five charges, resulting in three convictions and two guilty pleas.

Section 271 (Sexual Assault)

Because section 271 continues to be used very frequently in child sexual assault cases, it is also useful to examine the associated conviction rates in this report. Figure 4.3 indicates that the conviction rates for section 271 are similar or slightly higher than the conviction rates for section 151 (see Figure 4.2). The highest rate reported was 89 percent for Hamilton cases, and the lowest was 60 percent for Edmonton cases. The Calgary conviction rate was 81 percent, and no rates were available for Saskatchewan.

**Figure 4.2  Conviction Rates for Section 151(Sexual Interference) By Location**

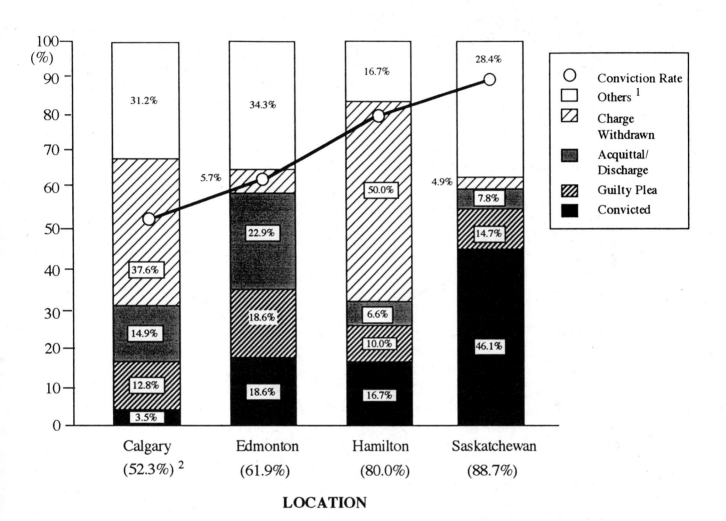

[1] "Others" for Calgary and Edmonton include stays, warrants, incomplete and trial pending. Stays, unknown, and trial pending are included in "Others" for Hamilton.

[2] Numbers in parentheses indicate conviction rates.

**Figure 4.3    Conviction Rates for Section 271(Sexual Assault) By Location**

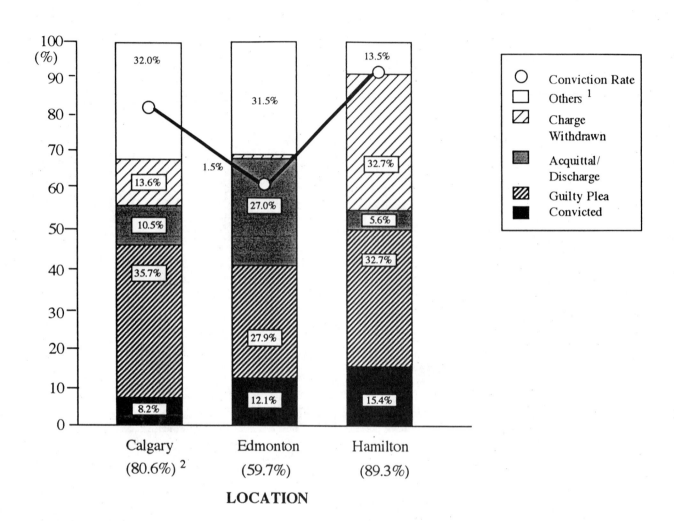

---

[1] "Others" for Calgary and Edmonton include stays, warrants, incomplete and trial pending. Stays, unknown, and trial pending are included in "Others" for Hamilton.

[2] Numbers in parentheses indicate conviction rates.

In general, the highest conviction rates are due to a very high proportion of the accused pleading guilty. The rate of guilty pleas was 36 percent for Calgary cases, 33 percent for Hamilton cases, and 28 percent for Edmonton cases. The Hamilton rate was also increased significantly by withdrawal of charges in 33 percent of the cases.

### 4.1.2 Objective # 2: To Provide More Protection for Young Victims

Another objective of Bill C-15 was to provide greater protection for young victims of sexual abuse. The following new sections relate to this objective: subsection 212(2), Living on the avails of a prostitute under 18 years; subsection 212(4), Obtaining a person under 18 years for sexual purpose; subsection 173(2), Indecent exposure to a child under 14 years for sexual purpose; section 150.1, Consent of child under 14 years old no defence; and subsection 150.1(2), Age difference and consent. In order to reflect on the extent to which this objective has been met, whether charges are being laid and what conviction rates are for subsections 212(2), 212(4), and 173(2) are examined below. Associated behaviour will also be examined for subsection 173(2). Further, the use of consent as a defence (section 150.1), as well as age difference and consent (subsection 150.1(2)), are examined.

<u>Charges Laid under Subsections 212(2) (Living On the Avails of a Prostitute Under 18 Years), 212(4) (Obtaining a Person Under 18 Years for Sexual Purpose), and 173(2) (Indecent Exposure to a Child Under 14 Years for Sexual Purpose)</u>

Subsections 212(2) (Living On the Avails of a Prostitute Under 18 Years) and 212(4) (Obtaining a Person Under 18 Years for Sexual Purpose)

In Calgary, Edmonton and Hamilton, no charges were laid under subsections 212(2) or 212(4) during the study period. In Saskatchewan, however, seven charges were laid under section 212 (no subsection available) in 1989. Unfortunately, no disposition data are available on these seven charges.

Anecdotal information suggests that subsection 212(2) is only enforceable when a prostitute "turns" against a pimp. Likewise, charges under subsection 212(4) can only be laid if the "John" is caught in the act. Thus, traditional police methods are not effective for enforcing subsections 212(2) and 212(4).

Subsection 173(2) (Indecent Exposure to a Child Under 14 Years for Sexual Purpose)

Disposition data indicate that relatively few charges were laid and concluded under subsection 173(2) during these studies. Edmonton police laid 26 charges under subsection 173(2) in a 31-month period, and Calgary police laid only two charges for the same time period. In Hamilton, police laid seven charges under this section during a one-year period and only three charges were laid in Saskatchewan in a 36-month period.

Behaviours Associated with Subsection 173(2) (Indecent Exposure to a Child Under 14 Years for Sexual Purpose)

Referring back to Table 4.1 indicates that data regarding behaviour associated with subsection 173(2) were available from police files on a few cases from Edmonton (n=22), Hamilton (n=7), and Saskatchewan (n=8), but no case information is available for Calgary. The common, and usually only, behaviour present with Edmonton and Hamilton cases was exposure (100 percent for both). The behaviour pattern for Saskatchewan cases, however, is more varied. Masturbation was the most frequently reported behaviour (50 percent), followed by exposure (25 percent) and invitation (25 percent).

Conviction Rates: Subsection 173(2) (Indecent Exposure to a Child Under 14 Years for Sexual Purpose)

For subsection 173(2), there were only two cases in Calgary and three in Saskatchewan where dispositions were recorded. Convictions were obtained in all cases. Data were available for seven cases in Hamilton, two of which resulted in convictions. The highest reliable rate, however, was 67 percent for Edmonton cases (n=26), and this conviction rate was due to a significant proportion of guilty pleas (i.e., 54 percent of all cases charged).

Application of Section 150.1 (Consent no Defence)

The data available did not permit a direct test of whether the courts accepted consent as a defence. However, data from preliminary inquiry and trial transcripts and/or tapes were available as to whether consent was raised by defence lawyers. Consent as a defence was raised most frequently in Calgary, where it was raised in almost one-half (48 percent) of the proceedings reviewed. It was also raised in 18 percent of the Edmonton proceedings, 16 percent of the Saskatchewan proceedings, and in only one of ten cases in Hamilton.

The proceedings reviewed also provided data on whether mistaken age was raised as a defence. The use of this type of defence was even less frequent than the reference to consent, discussed above. The largest proportion of cases at any site that involved mistaken age as a defence was nine percent for Calgary cases. Saskatchewan cases ranked next highest with five percent, and the review in Edmonton documented only one case.

### Application of Subsection 150.1(2) (Age Difference and Consent)

In cases where the complainant is at least 12 years of age, and the accused is not in a position of trust or authority, is 12 to 15 years of age, and is less than two years older than the complainant, consent as a defence may be used in criminal proceedings.

For both Calgary and Edmonton, only six cases were identified where age difference was relevant under subsection 150.1(2). All of these involved charges under section 271. One of these cases was concluded by a guilty plea, two by conviction, and three by acquittal.

In Saskatchewan three cases were identified that resulted in charges being laid and met the criteria of minimum age difference between the victim and the accused. One accused was charged under section 271, and the two other cases involved charges under sections 151 and 152, and subsection 173(2). No relevant cases were identified for Hamilton. Further, it was not possible to identify whether consent was used as a defence in any of the cases from any of the sites.

### 4.1.3 Objective # 3: To Eliminate Gender Bias Regarding Victims and Offenders

The new legislation was also designed to eliminate gender specific offences. Thus, sections 151, 152 and 153 refer to cases where "every person" who commits specific acts against "any person," omitting previous references to "male persons" and "female persons." To reflect on whether this objective has been achieved, it is useful to identify cases involving male victims and cases involving female offenders because these tend to be the minority type of cases.

Male Victims: Sections 151 (Sexual Interference), 152 (Invitation to Sexual Touching) and 153 (Sexual Exploitation)

For cases charged under section 151, over one-quarter of Hamilton's cases (i.e., 27 percent) involved male victims, compared to 16 percent for Saskatchewan cases and 14 percent for both Calgary and Edmonton cases. For cases charged under section 152, one of ten Calgary victims was male, five of 20 Edmonton victims were male, three of four Hamilton victims were male, and none of the seven Saskatchewan cases involved male victims. In terms of section 153, Hamilton police had ten of 13 cases which involved male victims, compared to one of three cases for Saskatchewan. Disposition data were not available for any cases involving charges under section 153 in Calgary or Edmonton. In terms of conviction rates, the number of cases involving male victims is so small that conviction rates would not be reliable.

Female Offenders: Sections 151 (Sexual Interference), 152 (Invitation to Sexual Touching) and 153 (Sexual Exploitation)

Neither Hamilton nor Calgary reported any cases involving female offenders that proceeded to disposition during the study period. In Edmonton, only one case involved a female offender charged under section 153. In Saskatchewan, disposition data were available on seven cases involving female offenders in which charges were laid under sections 151 and 153. Five charges were laid under section 151, and two charges were laid under section 153. Of the five cases charged under section 151, two of the female accused were convicted, two had charges discharged, and in one case the charge was stayed.

The small percentage of cases involving female offenders is somewhat unexpected since approximately five percent of the cases investigated by police in Calgary and two percent of the cases investigated in Edmonton involved female suspects. However, most of these cases seem to be screened out prior to laying charges. If we consider only cases where the police have cleared by charge, this proportion drops to less than two percent both in Calgary (n=6) and Edmonton (n=9).

4.1.4 Objective # 4: To Provide Protection for Children in Cases Where Disclosure is Delayed

The repeal of section 141, which provided for the one-year limitation for reporting certain sexual offences, and the abrogation of the doctrine of recent complaint with respect to all sexual offences (section 275 CC), enacted by Bill C-127 in August 1982, were aimed at protecting children in cases where disclosure was delayed.

The percentage of cases where the report to police occurred more than one year after the incident ranged from a high of 14 percent for Saskatchewan cases to a low of less than two percent for Edmonton cases. For Calgary and Hamilton, the proportions were six percent and nine percent respectively. In terms of conviction rates, all of the Hamilton cases (n=6) resulted in convictions, compared to a 77 percent conviction rate for Saskatchewan cases (n=155), and 60 percent for Calgary cases (n=14). None of the Edmonton cases were concluded by the end of the study. Although the number of relevant cases is limited, the findings suggest that a significant number of cases are resulting in charges, and the conviction rates for these charges compare favourably to conviction rates for cases where the report was made in less than one year, i.e., 70 percent for Calgary cases, and 93 percent for Hamilton cases. Comparable rates were not available for Saskatchewan cases.

## 4.2 Goal # 2: To Enhance Successful Prosecution of Child Sexual Abuse Cases

The findings relevant to Goal # 2 of Bill C-15 are presented below as they relate to Objectives # 5 and # 6.

### 4.2.1 Objective # 5: To Review the Problem of Child Sexual Abuse Victims Giving Evidence

The introduction of section 715.1 CC, permitting a videotape of the victim's description of events to be admissible in evidence, and subsection 16(1) of the Canada Evidence Act, allowing victims/witnesses under 14 years old to give testimony under oath or on a promise to tell the truth, were intended to facilitate the giving of evidence by children.

Section 715.1 (Videotaped Evidence)

Calgary

During the timeframe of the study, videotapes were made in only three of 731 cases investigated and reviewed. Audiotapes, however, were frequently made. None of the videotapes and audiotapes were used in evidence. However, one case investigated by the RCMP (R. v. Beauchamp and Beauchamp) was observed in court in Calgary and will be discussed later.

Edmonton

During the time period of the study, videotapes of the victim were made for 119 (18 percent) of the cases investigated by the Edmonton Police Service. However, very few were used in evidence. These are briefly discussed below.

The first case considering the use of videotaped evidence was R. v. Meddoui.[1] The trial judge was required to address two major issues: (a) what constituted "a reasonable time after the offence" for the making of the videotape and (b) what was required before the child could be said to have "adopted" the contents of the videotape. The trial judge held that the tape had been made within a reasonable time (two days after the offence date) and that the child had adopted its contents. This opinion was upheld on appeal.[2]

On February 27, 1989, the constitutional validity of section 715.1 was challenged in Alberta in R. v. Thompson.[3] McKenzie, J., ruled that the section violated the accused's rights under the Charter of Rights and Freedoms. Nevertheless, in this case, the accused was convicted. This decision appears to have effectively halted further attempts to use the videotape provisions at the Queen's Bench level until R. v. Beauchamp and Beauchamp.[4] In that case, the defence raised the same Charter issues as had been raised in Thompson. The argument was unsuccessful, the videotape was admitted and the accused were convicted on June 28, 1990. As neither of these cases were appealed, there are now conflicting opinions in the Alberta Court of Queen's Bench about the constitutional validity of the videotaped evidence section.

The only case to reach the Alberta Court of Appeal was the appeal from conviction in Meddoui.[5] The Court of Appeal did not discuss the constitutional validity of the section and made only a passing reference to the concerns raised by McKenzie, J., in Thompson. It is not clear whether the Court rejected the ruling in Thompson or whether, because the trial decision in Meddoui was rendered prior to Thompson when the validity of the section had not yet been challenged, the Court saw no need to consider that issue.

---

[1] R. v. Meddoui (unreported), Edmonton Registry, Nov. 1, 1988, Sinclair, J. (Alta. Q.B.).

[2] R. v. Meddoui (1991), 61 C.C.C. (3d) 345, 2 C.R. (4th) 316, 111 A.R. 295 (C.A.), Kerans, Harradence and Girgulis, JJ.A. A new trial was ordered for different reasons.

[3] R. v. Thompson (1989), 68 C.R. (3d) 328, 97 A.R. 157 (Alta. Q.B.).

[4] R. v. Beauchamp and Beauchamp (unreported), Calgary No. 8901-0707-CO, June 28, 1990, Power, J. (Alta. Q.B.).

[5] Supra, n. 2.

Hamilton

During the time frame of the study, the videotaping provisions of Bill C-15 were not being used because of the R. v. Thompson (1989) judgements discussed above. Hamilton-Wentworth police and the Children's Aid Societies, however, had begun to develop a protocol for videotaping the child's initial statement.

Saskatchewan

Police file data indicate that videotapes were made for 34 percent of the cases investigated during the 36-month time frame of the study. Victims disclosed the sexual abuse on videotape in 86 percent of the cases, and identified the offender on the videotape in 81 percent of the cases. Videotapes were used in evidence during the preliminary inquiry pursuant to section 643.1 in ten percent of the cases (n=10). In six cases a reason was given for requesting the videotape. The reasons were as follows: (a) reflection of the interview (two cases); (b) the videotape contradicted the statement given at the hearing (three cases); and (c) the child refused to disclose during the hearing (one case).

## Subsection 16(1) CEA (The Oath)

During court proceedings in Calgary, 76 percent of the victim/witnesses under 14 years old were sworn either directly (12 percent) or after questioning by the judge (63 percent), while the remainder of the children (25 percent) gave evidence under the promise to tell the truth provision. One-half of the Edmonton victim/witnesses under 14 years old were sworn. The other half gave evidence under a promise to tell the truth. In Hamilton, only five child victim/witnesses were observed during court proceedings; however, of these, four were sworn. No information on being sworn was available for Saskatchewan cases.

There was considerable consistency between the sites in terms of the types of questions asked by the judge while deciding whether to swear the child/witness, with the exception of Edmonton, where judges tended only to instruct the children and then swear them. In the other three locations, judges tended to ask a number of general questions (Saskatchewan - 87 percent, Hamilton - 80 percent, Calgary - 28 percent) and question the child regarding understanding of the meaning of the oath (Hamilton - 40 percent, Saskatchewan - 18 percent, Calgary - 14 percent). The child's knowledge of truth or lie was also frequently asked by judges in Hamilton (60 percent) and Calgary (32 percent). Only Saskatchewan judges tended to continue to ask questions concerning belief in God or religious belief (47 percent).

### 4.2.2 Objective # 6: To Protect the Credibility of the Child Victim/Witness in Cases of Child Abuse

The removal of the requirement for corroboration under section 274 CC for charges related to child sexual abuse and the exclusion of evidence of sexual activity (subsection 276(1) CC) and reputation (section 277 CC) of the victims is intended to protect the credibility of the child victim/witness.[6]

#### Section 274 (Corroboration Not Required)

While there are little data that reflect directly on the issue of the importance of corroboration -- given that corroboration is not required (section 274) -- some indirect information is relevant. First, the importance of the existence of witnesses may be considered an indication of corroboration. Witnesses would presumably support the testimony of the child witness. Second, if there is more than one victim giving testimony, the evidence of one child could be assumed to corroborate the testimony of another.

The findings presented in Figure 3.8 on the decision by police to lay charges provide some useful information regarding the issue of corroboration. First, for Calgary and Hamilton cases, the presence of witnesses, usually corroborative, was highly associated with the police laying charges. Witnesses were not as important in Edmonton cases, however, involvement of more than one victim in the case was an important factor in the determination that charges be laid.

The only data that were directly applicable to the importance of corroboration were obtained from the Saskatchewan preliminary inquiry review. For those cases discharged at preliminary inquiry, the judge commented on the lack of corroboration in 11 of 13 cases, and the lack of sexual contact in nine of 13 cases. Expert witnesses were used in nine percent of the Calgary cases, one percent of the Edmonton cases, and 11 percent of the Saskatchewan cases. Unfortunately, information is not available on what their testimony involved, or how it was used in the proceedings.

---

[6] All three of these provisions were originally enacted by Bill C-127 in August 1982. However, they were extended in the provisions established by Bill C-15.

<u>Subsection 276(1) (Sexual Activity) and Section 277 (Reputation)</u>[7]

Table 4.2 lists all the issues raised by defence lawyers in cross-examination by location. As the data indicate, the issue of past sexual conduct of the victim was most frequently raised in Saskatchewan, and this was in only nine percent of the cases. Otherwise it was seldom raised. Reputation of the victim was also seldom, if ever, brought up. In Calgary and Hamilton, for example, it was never raised. However, it was raised in 18 percent of the cases in Edmonton and four percent of the cases in Saskatchewan.

The issues that were raised by defence lawyers frequently were: (a) nature of conduct (Calgary - 70 percent, Hamilton - 70 percent, Saskatchewan - 25 percent, and Edmonton - 41 percent); (b) fabrication of allegation (Hamilton - 90 percent, Calgary - 39 percent, Saskatchewan - 31 percent, and Edmonton - 20 percent); and (c) circumstances of disclosure (Hamilton - 80 percent, Calgary - 57 percent, Edmonton - 37 percent, and Saskatchewan - 16 percent).

## 4.3  Goal # 3: To Improve the Experience of the Child Victim/Witness

The findings relevant to Goal # 3 of Bill C-15 are presented below as they relate to Objectives # 7, # 8, and # 9.

### 4.3.1  Objective # 7: To Avoid Repetitious Interviews with the Child Victim/Witness

One rationale for the introduction of section 715.1 CC (Permitting a videotape of the victim's description of event to be admissible in evidence) was to reduce the number of times that the child victim had to tell the story of the occurrence. Unfortunately, as discussed in Section 4.2.1 above, the videotapes were made mainly in Edmonton (18 percent of the cases) and Saskatchewan (34 percent of the cases). However, these videotapes were seldom used in court. The primary reason the videotapes were made was to aid the police in the investigation. Thus, no reliable information was available concerning whether having a videotape decreased the number of times the child had to describe the incident.

---

[7] On August 22, 1991, section 276 was struck down by the Supreme Court of Canada in <u>R</u>. v. <u>Seaboyer</u>; <u>R</u>. v. <u>Gayme</u>.

## Table 4.2   Issues Raised as Defence in Cross-Examination By Location[1]

| Issues Raised | Calgary | | Edmonton | | Hamilton | | Saskatchewan | |
|---|---|---|---|---|---|---|---|---|
| | n | % | n | % | n | % | n | % |
| Identity of accused | 9 | 39.1 | 2 | 4.1 | 0 | 0 | 26 | 18.6 |
| Nature of conduct | 16 | 69.6 | 20 | 40.8 | 7 | 70.0 | 35 | 25.0 |
| Consent to acts | 11 | 47.8 | 9 | 18.4 | 1 | 10.0 | 22 | 15.7 |
| No threats or force | 6 | 26.1 | 11 | 22.4 | 1 | 10.0 | 32 | 22.9 |
| No relationship of authority | 1 | 4.3 | 3 | 61.7 | 0 | 0 | 4 | 2.9 |
| Honest belief re: age | 2 | 8.7 | 1 | 2.0 | 1 | 10.0 | 5 | 3.6 |
| Use of drugs/alcohol - Accused | 1 | 4.3 | 5 | 10.2 | 2 | 20.0 | 20 | 14.3 |
| Use of drugs/alcohol - Victim | 0 | 0 | 9 | 18.4 | 2 | 2.0 | 17 | 12.1 |
| Provocation by victim | 6 | 26.1 | 1 | 2.0 | 0 | 0 | 8 | 5.7 |
| Past sexual conduct of victim | 1 | 4.3 | 3 | 6.1 | 0 | 0 | 13 | 9.3 |
| Reputation of victim | 0 | 0 | 9 | 18.4 | 0 | 0 | 6 | 4.3 |
| Fabrication of allegation | 9 | 39.0 | 10 | 20.4 | 9 | 90.0 | 44 | 31.4 |
| Inconsistent with prior testimony | 2 | 8.7 | 1 | 2.0 | 8 | 80.0 | 23 | 19.0 |
| Inconsistent with video tape | 0 | 0 | 0 | 0 | 0 | 0 | 3 | 2.1 |
| Validity of video tape | 0 | 0 | 0 | 0 | 0 | 0 | 1 | 0.7 |
| Circumstances of disclosure | 13 | 56.5 | 18 | 36.7 | 8 | 80.0 | 22 | 15.7 |
| Reasons for disclosure | 9 | 39.1 | 8 | 16.3 | 8 | 80.0 | 31 | 22.1 |
| Total number of cases reviewed | 23 | | 49 | | 10 | | 140 | |

---

[1] Source of data: Court proceedings review

### 4.3.2 Objective # 8: To Provide Support and Assistance to the Child Victim/Witness While Giving Testimony

Bill C-15 attempts to provide support and assistance to the child victim/witness in a number of ways. First, support can be provided by subsection 486(2.1) CC, which permits the child victim/witness to testify outside the courtroom or behind a screen. Second, support and assistance can be provided to the child through the exclusion of the public from the courtroom by subsection 486(1) CC. Nonlegislated supports, such as victim/witness assistance programs and preparation by the crown prosecutors, may also be available to the child victim/witness in some locations. All of these options are addressed below.

Victim/Witness Assistance Programs

During the time frame of the site studies, there were no victim/witness assistance programs for child sexual abuse victim/witnesses in Alberta or Saskatchewan. In contrast, the Hamilton victim/witnesses had access to a support program. This program is described in detail in the site report (Campbell et al.).

Preparation of the Victim/Witness by the Crown Prosecutors

Data were available concerning the activities of the crown prosecutors who prepared victim/witnesses for court in Hamilton, as well as in Calgary and Edmonton (grouped together).

Calgary and Edmonton

The vast majority (94 percent) of the crown prosecutors who responded to the mailed questionnaires in Alberta usually met with child victim/witnesses prior to court. In terms of what they did when they met with the child, 100 percent of the respondents indicated that they "explained the court process," followed by explaining the type of questions the crown prosecutor asks (97 percent), those the defence lawyer asks, explaining the oath (82 percent) and telling the child to inform them if the accused or spectators are intimidating (77 percent). In contrast to the common items, only one crown prosecutor mentioned explaining to the child that acquittal does not mean disbelief.

Hamilton

All the crown prosecutors surveyed for the Hamilton study (six respondents) met with a child victim/witness prior to court. The most common ways in which they prepared children were by explaining the following: the court process; the types of questions that the child may expect to be asked by both the defence lawyer and the crown prosecutor; and the oath-taking procedure. Five of the six also said they role-played the court appearance with the victim, but only three showed the child an actual courtroom. The least common preparations undertaken by crown prosecutors were introducing the child to the individuals who work in the court and providing the child with reading materials.

Subsection 486(2.1) (Testimony Outside the Courtroom)

Table 4.3 indicates that child victim/witnesses testified behind a screen in 24 percent of the court proceedings observed in Saskatchewan, as well as in nine percent of the Calgary proceedings. None of the Hamilton courts used the screen during court observations, however, other information indicates that it was used in some cases that were not observed. In addition to having the highest rate for utilization of the screen, Saskatchewan courts were also the only courts to use the closed-circuit television in 24 percent of the proceedings. The only other innovation used in a significant percentage of cases was support adults staying in court (Hamilton - 92 percent, Calgary - 75 percent, Edmonton - 48 percent, and Saskatchewan - 38 percent).

Subsection 486(1) (Exclusion of the Public)

Although subsection 486(1) predates Bill C-15, it is particularly relevant to sexual offences and is therefore included here. Request for exclusion of the public ranged from a high of 33 percent of the Hamilton court proceedings observed to a low of four percent for Saskatchewan cases. Request for exclusion was also made in 22 percent of the Calgary proceedings and 18 percent of the Edmonton proceedings. Once the requests were made, they were almost always ordered by the judge.

4.3.3   Objective # 9: To Provide Protection for the Child Victim/Witness Regarding Identity and Circumstances of the Occurrence

Subsection 486(3) CC allows for the protection of the identity of victims and witnesses in sexual offence cases by prohibiting the publication of information which might identify them. This is not an automatic ban and must be requested either by the crown prosecutor or the judge. The intent of this ban is to provide protection of the child victim/witness by preventing public knowledge of the child's identity and circumstances of the incident.

Request for ban on publication of the victim's identity under subsection 486(3) was requested in 90 percent of the Hamilton proceedings, 79 percent of the Saskatchewan proceedings, 61 percent of the Calgary proceedings, and 55 per

## Table 4.3    Courtroom Environment During the Child's Testimony[1]

| Items observed | Calgary n | Calgary % | Edmonton n | Edmonton % | Hamilton n | Hamilton % | Saskatchewan n | Saskatchewan % |
|---|---|---|---|---|---|---|---|---|
| Child testifies behind screen | 8 | 9.2 | 2 | 3.1 | 0 | 0 | 5 | 23.8 |
| Child testifies via closed-circuit television | 0 | 0 | 0 | 0 | 0 | 0 | 5 | 23.8 |
| Child given booster seat | 1 | 1.1 | 0 | 0 | 0 | 0 | 0 | 0 |
| Adult holds child on knee | 1 | 1.1 | 0 | 0 | 0 | 0 | 0 | 0 |
| Adult accompanies child to stand | 6 | 6.9 | 1 | 1.6 | 0 | 0 | 1 | 4.8 |
| Support adult stays in court room | 65 | 74.7 | 31 | 48.4 | 11 | 91.7 | 8 | 38.1 |
| Witnesses cleared during child's testimony | 72 | 82.7 | 62 | 96.9 | 7 | 70.0 | 13 | 61.9 |
| Accused cleared from court room | 0 | 0 | 0 | 0 | 0 | 0 | 0 | 0 |
| Spectators cleared from court room | 1 | 1.1 | 4 | 6.3 | 5 | 0 | 0 | 0 |
| Child allowed to turn from accused | 44 | 50.6 | 2 | 3.1 | 0 | 0 | 4 | 19.0 |
| Offender seated in back of court | 0 | 0 | 0 | 0 | 0 | 0 | 5 | 23.8 |
| Child's view of accused obstructed | 15 | 17.2 | 1 | 1.6 | 5 | 41.7 | 0 | 0 |
| Expert testifies re: Child's testimony | 7 | 8.0 | 0 | 0 | 0 | 0 | 0 | 0 |
| Child allowed to bring blanket, toy, etc. | 6 | 6.9 | 3 | 4.7 | 0 | 0 | 0 | 0 |
| Child allowed to testify with props | 1 | 1.1 | 4 | 6.3 | 0 | 0 | 0 | 0 |
| Other innovative procedures used dolls/pictures | 8 | 9.2 | 7 | 10.9 | 0 | 0 | 5 | 23.8 |
| Total number of cases observed | 87 | | 64 | | 12 | | 21 | |

---

[1] Source of data: Court Observation

cent of the Edmonton proceedings. The vast majority of all requests were ordered.

**4.4 Goal # 4: To Bring Sentencing in Line with the Severity of the Incident**

The findings relevant to Goal # 4 of Bill C-15 are presented below as they relate to Objective # 10.

4.4.1 Objective # 10: To Provide for a Range of Sentence Responses to a Broad Range of Severity of Abuse[8]

Consistent with the fact that, as discussed above, the new legislation is designed to cover a broad range of behaviour, most of the sections (specifically sections 151, 152, 153, 159, and 160 CC) are hybrid offences (i.e., summary or indictable offences). Thus, the range of sentencing alternatives is also broad in order to bring the sentencing in line with the severity of the incident.

The findings presented in Section 4.1 above identified two very clear trends which set the parameters for the data analysis of this section. First, section 151 (Sexual interference for children under 14) is the only section of the new codes introduced by Bill C-15 which obtained sufficient frequencies for detailed analysis. Second, both the frequency and changes in the rates of charging for section 271 (Sexual assault) indicate that it plays a significant part in the overall response to child sexual abuse. Therefore, this section of the report will focus the sentencing analysis on both sections 151 and 271. Information is first presented on the specific types of dispositions for sections 151 and 271.

Dispositions for Section 151 (Sexual Interference)

Calgary

Figure 4.4 contains a breakdown of disposition types for sections 151 and 271, and Figure 4.5 presents the breakdown of incarceration times for sections 151 and 271. In terms of section 151, the most common disposition for Calgary cases was incarceration (30 percent) and incarceration with probation (30 percent), which results in a total incarceration rate of 60 percent. The next most common sentence was suspended sentence and probation, at 28 percent. Incarceration

---

[8] Unfortunately comparable data are only available for Calgary and Edmonton. Thus, no information will be included in this section from the Hamilton or Saskatchewan studies. The incarceration rate for section 151 in Saskatchewan was 62 percent.

**Figure 4.4  Dispositions for Sections 151 and 271 in Calgary and Edmonton**

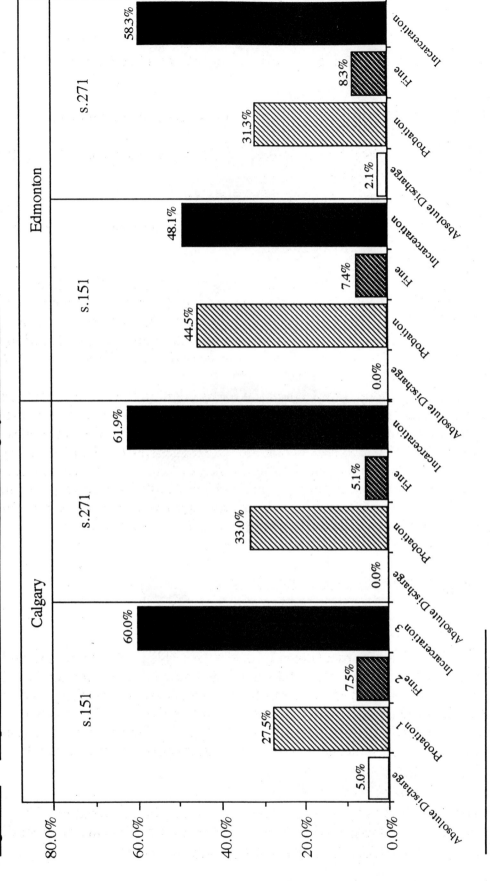

[1] Probation includes "Conditional Discharge and Probation," "Suspended Sentence and Probation," and "Unspecified Probation."

[2] Fine includes "Fine," and "Fine & Probation."

[3] Incarceration includes "Incarceration," "Incarceration with Probation," and "Intermittent Jail."

**Figure 4.5** <u>Incarceration Times for Sections 151 and 271 in Calgary and Edmonton</u>

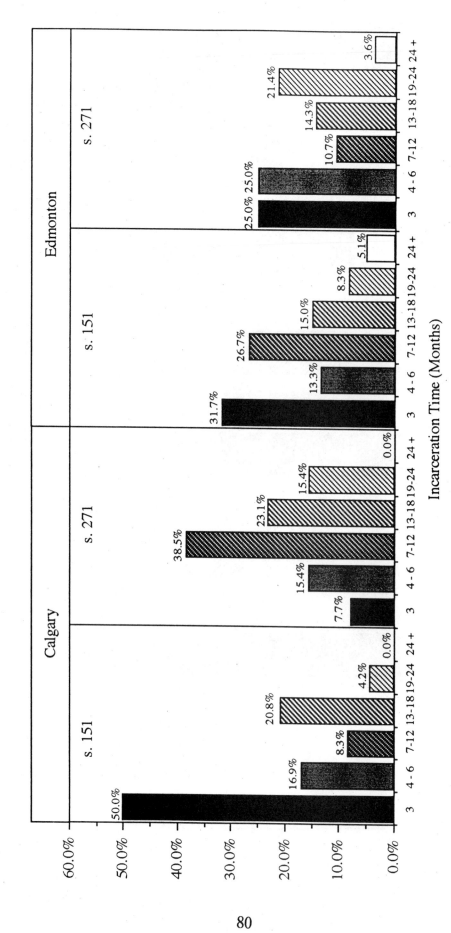

was three months or less in 50 percent of the cases, followed by 13 to 18 months (21 percent) and four to six months (17 percent). The average incarceration time for section 151 was 6.7 months.

Edmonton

The most common disposition for Edmonton cases for section 151 was incarceration. The total rate of incarceration amounted to 48 percent, and probation accounted for 45 percent. Of those incarcerated, the most common sentence was three months or less (32 percent). The second largest category of incarceration was seven to 12 months (27 percent) and 13 to 18 months (15 percent). The average incarceration time for section 151 was 11.1 months.

Dispositions for Section 271 (Sexual Assault)

Calgary

Dispositions for section 271 are somewhat similar to section 151 for Calgary cases. The incarceration rate was 62 percent of all dispositions. The next highest category was probation at 33 percent. The most frequent sentence involving incarceration was seven to 12 months for 39 percent of those incarcerated; the next most frequent sentence was 13 to 18 months (23 percent). The average time of incarceration for section 271 was 9.9 months.

Edmonton

Dispositions for section 271 are also similar to section 151 for Edmonton cases. Incarceration was ordered in 58 percent of the convictions, and various types of probation accounted for the remaining cases. The most common lengths of incarceration were three months or less (25 percent) and four to six months (25 percent), followed by 19 to 24 months (21 percent) and 13 to 18 months for 14 percent of those incarcerated. The average incarceration time for section 271 was 11.2 months.

## 4.5 Summary

### 4.5.1 Goal # 1: To Provide Better Protection to Child Sexual Abuse Victim/Witnesses

The findings relevant to Goal # 1 of Bill C-15 are listed below.

- The number of charges under sections of Bill C-15, especially section 151, was high and increased over time. The number of charges laid under section 271 (Sexual assault) was also high.

- Conviction rates for most sections were high.

- Guilty plea rates were high, especially for section 271 (Sexual assault).

- A broad range of conduct is being covered by sections 151, 152, 153 and 271.

- Many cases (20 to 30 percent) involved male victims, and some female offenders are being charged.

- There were few charges laid under subsection 212(2) (Living on the avails) and subsection 212(4) (Obtaining for sexual purposes).

### 4.5.2 Goal # 2: To Enhance Successful Prosecution of Child Sexual Abuse Cases

The findings relevant to Goal # 2 of Bill C-15 are listed below.

- Videotaping was found to be useful for police investigations and refreshing the child's memory prior to proceedings, as was the case in R. v. Beauchamp and Beauchamp in Calgary.

- In proceedings, the child victim/witness was usually sworn, especially if they were over 12 years of age.

- If the child was not sworn, evidence was taken under the promise to tell the truth.

- Corroboration still seems important for laying charges, but was not found to be related to conviction.

- Some expert witnesses are being used, especially with younger children.

- R. v. Thompson limited the use of videotapes as evidence during the time of the site studies.

- In the few cases where videotapes were used, the child was still extensively cross-examined.

### 4.5.3 Goal # 3: To Improve the Experience of the Child Victim/Witness

The findings relevant to Goal # 3 of Bill C-15 are listed below.

- Support adults were often present during proceedings.

- Ban on publication (subsection 486(3)) was widely used in all jurisdictions.

- The witness was usually allowed to turn away from the accused. In some jurisdictions this was facilitated by the layout of the courtroom.

- Screens and closed-circuit television were seldom used.

### 4.5.4 Goal # 4: To Bring Sentencing in Line with the Severity of the Offence

The findings relevant to Goal # 4 of Bill C-15 are listed below.

- Incarceration rates for section 151 (Sexual interference) and section 271 (Sexual assault) were high, ranging from 48 percent (for section 151 in Edmonton) to a high of 62 percent (for section 271 in Calgary).

- Time of incarceration for section 271 was slightly higher than for section 151 (section 151 = 6.7 months in Calgary and 11.1 months in Edmonton compared to section 271 = 9.9 months in Calgary and 11.2 months in Edmonton).

- Sentencing data were limited. Comparison and/or trend data are needed to reflect on the issue of sentencing.

# 5.0 PERCEPTIONS OF PROFESSIONALS, CHILD VICTIMS AND PARENTS REGARDING BILL C-15, <u>AN ACT TO AMEND THE CRIMINAL CODE AND THE CANADA EVIDENCE ACT</u>

This chapter focusses on professionals' perceptions of problems, changes, and effects of provisions of Bill C-15. The presented data were collected through a self-administered key informant survey described in Chapter 2.0.[1] This information is most relevant to the third purpose of the site studies:

(3) to identify the degree to which the goals and objectives of Bill C-15 have been achieved.

The information presented is based on professionals' perceptions and is intended to augment the quantitative data presented in Chapter 4.0 regarding the impact of Bill C-15. The professional groups responding at the various sites included social workers, police, crown prosecutors, defence lawyers and judges. Data were gathered from a total of 48 judges (Alberta=18, Hamilton=8, Saskatchewan=22), 58 crown prosecutors (Alberta=35, Hamilton=6, Saskatchewan=17), 37 defence lawyers (Alberta=24, Hamilton=3, Saskatchewan=10), and 75 police officers (Alberta=45, Hamilton=6, Saskatchewan=24). Social workers' perceptions were not recorded in Saskatchewan. It is not suggested that the findings in this chapter represent the professional groups. One should be cautious in generalizing the views and experiences discussed below as reflecting any professional group's perceptions of Bill C-15. However, the data presented in this chapter do provide insights into professionals' thinking and identify issues of Bill C-15 that might be relevant.

## 5.1 Perceived Problems With Substantive Sections of Bill C-15

General comments relevant to substantive issues specific to individual charges of Bill C-15 are summarized below. The information presented has been obtained from an open-ended question that asked judges, crown prosecutors, defence lawyers, and police officers to identify problems they perceived with those sections of the <u>Criminal Code</u> enacted because of Bill C-15.

An overall review of the findings from the various site reports regarding the substantive aspect of Bill C-15 indicates that there was not much agreement

---

[1] The Hamilton study relied on personal interviews to collect the views of judges on the impact of Bill C-15.

among the individual respondents regarding perceived problems. Only a few trends emerged and are summarized by specific <u>Criminal Code</u> section below.

### 5.1.1 Issues Related to Specific Sections

<u>Section 151 (Sexual Interference)</u>

Three issues were raised by a small number of the respondents. They are as follows: (a) it is difficult to differentiate sexual interference (section 151) from sexual assault (section 271); (b) "sexual touching" is difficult to define; and (c) a long time lapse from incident to report could be a problem.

<u>Section 153 (Sexual Exploitation)</u>

The lack of clarity of the definition of "a person in a position of trust or authority" was reported to be a problem with sexual exploitation (section 153).

<u>Subsection 212(2) (Living on the Avails of Prostitution)</u>

Both crown prosecutors and policemen indicated that the problem with subsection 212(2) was getting the victim to testify.

## 5.2 Reported Experience With Procedural Items Related to Bill C-15[2]

The self-reported experiences of crown prosecutors, defence lawyers, and judges with the various procedural components relevant to Bill C-15 that provide support for child/victims while giving testimony in court are discussed below. These include testimony outside the courtroom (subsection 486(2.1)), ban on publication (subsection 486(3)), and videotaped evidence (section 715.1). In addition, a number of other procedural items not formally part of Bill C-15 were included in the analysis since they were thought to aid the child victim/witness in giving testimony. Respondents indicated whether a request had been made for an item, whether objections had been heard, and whether the item had been subsequently allowed.

There was overall consistency in perceptions and requests of items. First, a comparison of response distributions across the three study sites indicates that similar items were requested. Crown prosecutors, defence lawyers and judges,

---

[2] See Tables B-8 to B-10 in Appendix B.

regardless of location, were fairly consistent in what procedural components they reported were most often requested, objected to or allowed. Ban on publication, support adult in court, witnesses cleared and spectators cleared were consistently the most frequently requested items. Other frequently requested procedural supports, particularly in Saskatchewan courts and to a lesser extent in Alberta courts, included: child sits on knee; adult accompanied to stand; videotape; screens; and props.

### 5.2.1 Perceptions of Crown Prosecutors[3]

Crown prosecutors were asked to respond to a series of questions. First, they were asked what procedural supports they had requested. Second, if available, did the defence lawyer object to their request, and finally, was their request allowed in court. Overall there was a high degree of consistency among crown prosecutors across all study sites regarding the types of requests they make. Ban on publication (Alberta - 100 percent, Hamilton - 100 percent, Saskatchewan - 100 percent), support adult in court (Alberta - 94 percent, Hamilton - 83 percent, Saskatchewan - 82 percent), witnesses cleared (Alberta - 94 percent, Hamilton - 67 percent, Saskatchewan - 65 percent) and spectators cleared (Alberta - 91 percent, Hamilton - 67 percent, Saskatchewan - 65 percent) were the most frequently requested procedures by crown prosecutors in all three locations. Adult accompanied child to stand (Alberta - 51 percent, Saskatchewan - 77 percent), use of screens (Alberta - 49 percent, Saskatchewan - 59 percent) and videotapes (Alberta - 37 percent, Saskatchewan - 41 percent), were frequently requested by Alberta and Saskatchewan crown prosecutors. Requests for microphones and props were frequently made in Saskatchewan (59 percent).

Crown prosecutors' requests were often objected to by defence lawyers. Crown prosecutors in Alberta and Saskatchewan reported that the majority of their requests to allow a child to sit on the knee of an adult while testifying (Alberta - 88 percent, Saskatchewan - 100 percent), allowing an adult to accompany the child to the stand (Alberta - 61 percent, Saskatchewan - 54 percent) and clearing spectators from the court before the child's testimony (Alberta - 59 percent, Saskatchewan - 64 percent) were challenged by defence lawyers. Alberta crown prosecutors also reported that most of their requests to videotape a child's testimony (85 percent), to use screens to shield a child during testimony (53 percent), and to allow an expert to testify about the significance of a child's testimony (57 percent), were objected to by defence lawyers. Saskatchewan crown prosecutors stated that defence lawyers objected to almost

---

[3] See Table B-8 in Appendix B.

two-thirds (64 percent) of their requests to have witnesses cleared from the court before the child gave testimony.

Crown prosecutors from Alberta and Saskatchewan reported judges allowed the vast majority of their requests, regardless of their nature. They stated that approximately 70 to 100 percent of their requests for ban on publication, adult accompanied to stand, support adult in court, witnesses cleared, and spectators cleared were allowed by the court. Similar rates of judges allowing a request were reported for most other procedural items. Crown prosecutors reported that their requests to allow a child to sit on the knee of an adult while testifying were least likely to be allowed by the court (Alberta - 50 percent, Saskatchewan - 60 percent).

5.2.2 Perceptions of Defence Lawyers[4]

Defence lawyers' responses to what requests were made, challenged, and allowed were similar to those of crown prosecutors. Defence lawyers most frequently reported requests on ban on publication (Alberta - 92 percent, Hamilton - 100 percent, Saskatchewan - N/A), support adult in court (Alberta - 67 percent, Hamilton - 100 percent, Saskatchewan - 80 percent), witnesses cleared (Alberta - 71 percent, Hamilton - 33 percent, Saskatchewan - 70 percent), spectators cleared (Alberta - 67 percent, Hamilton - 33 percent, Saskatchewan - 40 percent) and, in Alberta and Saskatchewan, requests for screens (29 percent and 60 percent respectively). Alberta and Saskatchewan defence lawyers also reported crown prosecutors in their provinces requesting videotapes (Alberta - 13 percent, Saskatchewan - 60 percent) and screens (Alberta - 29 percent, Saskatchewan - 60 percent).

Defence lawyers reported challenging relatively few crown prosecutors' requests. This finding is of some interest given the views of crown prosecutors on how often their requests were objected to by defence lawyers. In contrast, defence lawyers' perceptions were consistent with those of crown prosecutors in agreeing that judges are more inclined to allow a request than to disallow it. Alberta and Hamilton defence lawyers reported very high rates of judges allowing a request no matter its nature. Saskatchewan defence lawyers, although reporting high rates of approval for most crown prosecutor requests, reported lower rates of approval for allowing supporting adults in the courtroom (50 percent) and for requests to clear spectators from the courtroom before the child gives testimony (57 percent).

---

[4] See Table B-9 in Appendix B.

### 5.2.3 Perceptions of Judges[5]

As with crown prosecutors and defence lawyers, the most frequently cited requests reported by judges were: ban on publication, support adult in court, witnesses cleared, and spectators cleared. Alberta and Saskatchewan judges also reported a number of requests for screens and videotapes. In addition, Saskatchewan judges reported frequent requests to allow a child to testify while turned away from the accused, to use microphones to amplify a child's voice, to bring toys, blankets, etc., into court, and to use booster seats.

Consistent with the previous findings mentioned above, judges reported approving almost all requests regardless of their nature. Judges in Alberta and Saskatchewan reported approving all requests for videotapes, screens, allowing a child to sit on the knee of an adult while testifying, allowing a child to testify turned away from the accused, and expert interpreters. In Saskatchewan, judges also allowed all requests for the use of toys, allowing adults to accompany a child to the stand, the use of microphones and closed-circuit television, and the use of experts to testify about the significance of a child's testimony.

In summary, an overall review of crown prosecutors', defence lawyers', and judges' responses suggests three patterns of requested items. The first pattern includes a group of items frequently requested by crown prosecutors, seldom objected to by defence lawyers, and allowed most of the time by judges. Ban on publication, support adult in court, and witnesses cleared all clearly fall into this group.

The second pattern of items includes those which crown prosecutors requested some of the time, were objected to frequently by defence lawyers, but usually allowed by judges. These items include videotape, child sits on knee, and adult accompanied child to stand.

A third and final group of items included those that were requested occasionally, not objected to, and usually allowed. These items include the use of booster seats and allowing the child the comfort of a toy.

## 5.3 Perceived Changes Due to Bill C-15

Respondents to the key informant survey were asked if they had observed changes in various areas relevant to the new provisions resulting from the

---

[5] See Table B-10 in Appendix B.

introduction of Bill C-15. Data were collected in all study sites from police officers, crown prosecutors, defence lawyers and judges.[6] Police officers from the three study sites agreed that changes have taken place, however, they differed on the nature of the changes. The most notable changes cited by police officers in Saskatchewan were the increase in the number of cases (67 percent) and the decreased need for corroboration (38 percent). Many Alberta and Hamilton police officers (50 percent) also reported an increase in the number of cases. As well, Alberta and Hamilton police officers reported that, because of Bill C-15, they felt the number of children giving evidence increased (Alberta - 22 percent, Hamilton - 33 percent). Some Alberta police officers (16 percent) also felt that children are testifying more and are being sworn at younger ages.

Crown prosecutors, more so than their judicial colleagues, reported Bill C-15 has resulted in an increase in the number of abuse cases coming to their attention. More than half (59 percent) of Saskatchewan, and one-third (33 percent) of Hamilton and Calgary (29 percent) crown prosecutors reported dealing with more cases of sexual abuse. High proportions of Saskatchewan's crown prosecutors (59 percent) also reported an increase in the number of children giving evidence and testifying at a younger age. Additionally, they felt the court was imposing harsher sentences (47 percent). The greatest change reported by Calgary crown prosecutors (40 percent) was in dropping the requirement for corroboration. Almost one-third (29 percent) of Calgary crown prosecutors also felt that children were testifying at a younger age due to amendments in the Bill. Hamilton crown prosecutors reported more children being required to testify under oath (67 percent), an increase in the use of eye witnesses (50 percent), and an elimination of the requirement for corroboration (50 percent).

Except for reporting an increase in the number of younger children testifying in their courts, the perceptions of judges in Alberta, Hamilton and Saskatchewan regarding changes due to Bill C-15 were mixed. Changes most often reported by Hamilton judges included children being sworn (38 percent), testifying at younger ages (25 percent), and an increased use of giving testimony under oath (25 percent). Saskatchewan judges reported an increase in the number of children giving evidence in their courts (50 percent). Alberta judges observed an increase in the number of younger children testifying, and reported an increase in the number of younger children who were being required to provide sworn testimony (28 percent).

---

[6] Data from social workers were also collected in Alberta and Hamilton, but few responded.

Defence lawyers' perceptions of changes due to Bill C-15 varied more than those of the other professionals. Likewise, defence lawyers did not tend to share the views of the other professionals. The most frequently recorded changes reported by Alberta defence lawyers were no longer requiring corroboration (25 percent), and the use of unsworn testimony for younger children - promise to tell the truth (21 percent). Hamilton defence lawyers reported the most changes, notably the use of rules of hearsay (67 percent) and weighting sworn versus unsworn evidence (67 percent). Saskatchewan defence lawyers commented that they observed an increase in the number of harsh sentences (50 percent), children testifying at younger ages (50 percent), and an increase in the number of judges who demonstrate better understanding when dealing with child witnesses (40 percent).

## 5.4 Impact Of Testifying On The Child

Survey participants were asked to respond to the open-ended question: "In your experience, what is the overall impact of the justice system on children who were required to testify in sexual assault cases?" In response to this question, most Alberta and Saskatchewan respondents, regardless of their professional affiliation, felt that giving testimony in court was a traumatic experience for children. Social workers (Alberta - 55 percent, Saskatchewan - N/A), police officers (Alberta - 51 percent, Saskatchewan - 58 percent) and crown prosecutors (Alberta - 49 percent, Saskatchewan - 53 percent) expressed similar levels of concern on this issue, whereas defence lawyers (Alberta - 25 percent, Saskatchewan - 40 percent) and judges (Alberta - 22 percent, Saskatchewan - 18 percent), although also reporting concern, were not as strong in their beliefs that testifying was "worse than the sexual abuse." In contrast to these findings, the next most often cited impact of testifying on the child was the feeling that it could have a positive effect. Some crown prosecutors, defence lawyers and judges in Saskatchewan, and a defence lawyer and judges in Hamilton reported they felt the act of testifying had little effect on children. Defence lawyers and judges in Saskatchewan tended to report that they did not know what the effects of testimony were on children.

## 5.5 Effect of Bill C-15 On the Professionals

### 5.5.1 Effects on The Job

An important issue relevant to the introduction of Bill C-15 is the extent to which it has affected the amount of work or the way professionals perform their roles. Most respondents felt that Bill C-15 made "no difference" in the way they performed their professional roles. While Bill C-15 has not changed their perception of their roles, many professionals felt it increased their workload. For example, many Alberta and Saskatchewan crown prosecutors (Alberta - 29 percent, Saskatchewan - 41 percent) and Saskatchewan police officers (29 percent) and judges (23 percent) reported their work loads had increased since the introduction of Bill C-15. However, when asked to comment on the number of cases being handled, most report there has been no change in the size of their caseloads. Only Calgary crown prosecutors (14 percent) and police officers (nine percent) reported an increase in the number of cases going to court. One-third of Saskatchewan crown prosecutors reported that cases were easier to prosecute, while almost two-thirds (60 percent) of defence lawyers commented that it was more difficult to prepare a defence because of Bill C-15. More than one-half (59 percent) of Saskatchewan's crown prosecutors also reported limited access to screens. In Hamilton, the largest, and perhaps most significant change, was reported by police officers. Four of six police respondents stated that it is now easier to prosecute cases in which younger children are implicated. Finally, defence lawyers from Calgary (21 percent) complained that trials were longer and more complicated.

### 5.5.2 Policy

The professionals were questioned concerning the extent to which they were aware of special policies and/or protocols specific to Bill C-15 for dealing with child sexual abuse cases.[7] In general, most professionals were not aware of any special policies or procedural changes resulting from Bill C-15. Of the professionals, however, police officers most frequently reported awareness of special policies/protocols. Over three-fourths of the Hamilton (83 percent) and Saskatchewan (75 percent) police officers said they were aware that special policies/protocols were in place. Crown prosecutors (Alberta - 29 percent, Hamilton - 17 percent, Saskatchewan - 53 percent) and social workers (Alberta - 23 percent, Hamilton - 67 percent), although to a lesser extent, also reported being aware of special policies and protocols specific to cases involving child sexual abuse.

---

[7] Comparable data from social workers in Saskatchewan, defence lawyers in Alberta and judges in Hamilton are not available and thus are not referred to in this section.

### 5.5.3 Training

Information regarding professionals' awareness and participation in training related specifically to Bill C-15 was also collected. Most respondents reported they were not aware of any specialized training opportunities available to them regarding Bill C-15. Of those expressing awareness of specialized training opportunities, however, social workers (92 percent), crown prosecutors (50 percent), and police officers (83 percent) in Hamilton were the most aware. In contrast, few Alberta or Saskatchewan professionals reported awareness of Bill C-15 specific training opportunities. Of interest, however, is that almost without exception all professionals, regardless of site, reported that when training was made available they participated in it.

## 5.6 Perceptions Of Child Victim/Witnesses in Alberta[8]

Seven children were interviewed after court proceedings were completed. All seven had been to court, and six of these children actually testified in court. Four were from the urban sites, and three were from the rural sites.

### 5.6.1 Court Preparation

Two of the children stated that they had attended scheduled precourt visits, one conducted by the crown prosecutor and a police officer together, and the other conducted by the crown prosecutor and a therapist. The other five children reported no precourt visit. The two children who attended precourt visits thought the visit helped them to know where they were going, and what the court looked like.

The children who described what the crown prosecutor did (n=4) all stated that the crown prosecutor was on their side; one stated that the crown prosecutor protects the innocent; and one stated that the crown prosecutor "protects me." Six of the seven children stated that the crown prosecutor explained what would happen in court. Four of these children remember the crown prosecutor explaining that they should tell the truth, and three remember being told to give definite answers. Most of the children (n=4) thought this helped them a little bit, and one thought it helped a lot. These children's responses show an alliance with the crown prosecutors and the importance of precourt meetings with the crown prosecutor in order to help the children feel prepared and supported.

---

[8] Comparable data are not available from the Hamilton or Saskatchewan studies.

Six of the seven children also had at least one support adult in addition to the crown prosecutor -- either a parent or guardian (in three cases), a social worker (in three cases), or a therapist or other family member. One way support adults helped was by telling the children that it was normal to feel frightened. Three children thought this helped quite a bit, and two thought it helped a little. This suggests the importance of supportive adults in the process and the importance of validating and normalizing the children's feelings of fear.

### 5.6.2 What Victim/Witnesses Would Tell Other Children

When the children were asked how they would help to prepare another child for court, the most common response was that they would advise the child to tell the truth (n=5). Other responses included general encouragement such as: be confident, be brave, don't be afraid, believe in yourself, and it will be fine (n=4). Other advice given by the children included: it's not your fault, ask questions if you don't understand, it will take a long time, the person may not be punished, it gets frustrating but go ahead, don't let them force words in your mouth, even if you lose he will get caught eventually, and it will be scary but you should tell so that it doesn't happen to someone else.

### 5.6.3 Testimony Experience

The general consensus of the child victim/witnesses was that the judge was there to listen to testimonies and make decisions about the guilt or innocence of the accused. One child stated that "the judge was there to protect you." Most of the children (n=4) felt the judge understood them a little bit. One felt well understood, and another felt not at all understood.[9] The children thought judges could improve their questions by using "normal language," by not being so aggressive, and by listening to their story more closely.

Most of the children felt understood by the crown prosecutor. Of the six that testified, four felt the crown prosecutor understood them quite a bit, one felt well understood, and one felt not at all understood. Three children thought the crown prosecutor's questions were confusing or not specific enough. One child did not feel comfortable asking for an explanation when it was needed.

---

[9] This was a case where the charges were dismissed at the preliminary hearing and the child was extremely angry.

Generally, the children were more negative about the cross-examination. Three of the five children who were cross-examined felt that the defence lawyer did not understand them at all, and two felt a bit understood. The type of comments made were that the defence lawyer was too aggressive (n=2), many questions were confusing and should not be asked twice, and the defence lawyer did not listen to them.

Four children felt that having family members in the courtroom made it easier for them to testify. One child even pretended she was talking to them while testifying. Another child felt more secure with the judge and the police in the courtroom so that the accused could not hurt her. Three children felt that having other people (except family members) in the courtroom made it harder for them to testify. Generally, having family members in the courtroom gave the children a lot of support during the testimony. There is some indication that the presence of authority figures offered the children security, but that the presence of strangers seemed to increase stress.

Two children brought objects (i.e., one wore her favourite pants, and one brought a rosary), which they felt were helpful to have with them. Three of the children thought having a favourite object in court might have been helpful. No screens were used in these cases, but three children thought it might have made the testimony easier. None of the children sat in chairs while testifying -- all stood. One eight-year old boy said he got very tired standing and would have liked to sit down.

### 5.6.4 General Comments About the Court Process

The children described a range of feelings about the court process: one child was generally happy; three were neither happy nor sad; and two had sad feelings. It appears these overall feelings about the court process were strongly influenced by the outcome, because the two children who felt very sad were witnesses in cases where the accused was either acquitted or the charges were dismissed. Both of these children described intense feelings of anger and a perception that no one had believed them. Other children made general comments that the whole process took much too long, that they had to tell their story too many times, and that they did not understand what an acquittal was. One child thought it was good for her to be able to tell her father (the accused) what she thought of him in court.

## 5.7 Perceptions of Parents/Guardians in Alberta[10]

Seven parents or guardians were interviewed after court proceedings using the structured interview schedules. Four were from urban sites and three were from rural sites. Victim/witnesses testified in six of these cases; in one case, the charges were dismissed, so the child, although present in court, did not testify.

### 5.7.1 Respondents

Two of the respondents were guardians of government wards; the remaining respondents were parents. Four of the respondents had completed high school and one had completed an undergraduate degree. Five of the respondents had annual incomes under $15,000. Four respondents were employed full time, and one respondent was employed part time. Marital statuses represented by this group included single, married, divorced and common law.

### 5.7.2 Social Workers

Parents/guardians reported that social workers were involved in five of the seven cases. In all five cases, social workers provided such services as: information or referral to other support services; follow-up services after the trial; financial assistance; the opportunity for the children to discuss their feelings about the trial; police liaison; and assistance with further counselling. In a few cases the social worker also provided information about the police investigation and court proceedings and likewise accompanied the child to the trial. Twenty-six of thirty-five specific social work interventions (74 percent) were rated as helpful by responding parents and guardians.

Parents/guardians reported that social workers alone interviewed four of the children about the sexual abuse incident. The other two children were interviewed by police and a social worker together. The interviewers were considered to be sensitive and able to communicate at the child's level in all cases rated by the parents/guardians.

---

[10] Comparable data are not available from the Hamilton or Saskatchewan studies.

### 5.7.3 Police

All parents/guardians reported that police provided them with information about the nature of the investigation and the court process. In most cases, police were also reported to have provided support and information about case outcome. In a minority of cases, the police reportedly referred victims to agencies or services. The police were found by parents and guardians to be most helpful in the areas of providing support around the sexual abuse, liaising with the crown prosecutor, and providing general information about the court process. The police were found to be helpful in 69 percent of the rated services they provided (24 of 35 police interventions).

Six respondents answered the remaining questions about police involvement. In all six cases, police interviewed the children within a few days of the report being made. In all six cases, the police were considered to be sensitive and able to communicate at the child's level.

### 5.7.4 Crown Prosecutors

Of the six reported cases, one parent/guardian respondent found the crown prosecutor helpful; the remaining responses ranged from not helpful to neither helpful nor unhelpful. The crown prosecutors were found to be helpful in 45 percent of the rated services they provided (18 of 42 specific services).

In terms of the specific services provided directly to respondents by the crown prosecutors, those offered most frequently were information about court dates, case status, court roles and process, the meaning of an oath, and the rules of testimony. Only one crown prosecutor conducted a courtroom tour. The crown prosecutors were found to be most helpful when they provided information about the meaning of an oath, the rules of testimony and court dates, appearances and scheduling. The respondents seemed to find the crown prosecutors to be most helpful with regard to the purely legal aspects of the crown prosecutor's role, that is, aspects that could not be provided by other professionals.

Six of the seven respondents felt that they did not have enough contact with the crown prosecutor. Of the five that observed the crown prosecutor's interview with the child, three felt that the communication was at the child's level and two did not. No referrals were made by the crown prosecutor to other services or organizations.

### 5.7.5 General Impact of Investigation/Reporting

Special techniques were reported to be used to gather evidence in two cases. They included the use of drawings by the child and tape recordings. According to the parents/guardians, the children were required to tell their story about the sexual abuse incident an average of six times (range = four to eight times).

The impact of the reporting and investigation process was reported to be negative on the child in four of the six reported cases. When asked how the reporting and investigation process could be made easier for the child, two respondents felt that the disclosure should have been videotaped. One respondent felt that there were too many professionals involved, and one respondent felt that the parents should be allowed to sit in on the interviews with the child. One respondent stated that no one in the process addressed the emotional needs of the child, and another thought that the police investigation took too long.

### 5.7.6 Trial Information

In two of the six cases, there was a special room for the victim and the victim's mother in which to wait prior to court. In another case, where such a room was not available, the family of the accused sat in the same waiting area making "rude remarks," which made the victim feel uncomfortable. Special assistance was given in only one case when the courtroom was closed to the public during the victim's testimony. Three of the respondents were in the room for the child's whole testimony, and three were not in the room for any of the testimony.

In terms of the overall court process, most respondents felt neutral about the questioning of themselves and their child by the police and the crown prosecutors. However, they felt quite uncomfortable with the questioning when it occurred during the court proceedings.

The respondents thought, on the average, that their children responded most favourably to police questioning, taking the oath, and talking to the crown prosecutor about the case. In contrast, they felt that their children were very uncomfortable giving evidence at the trial, being cross-examined, recalling the sexual abuse incident, and having the accused present in court.

Three of the seven children later expressed fears to the parents/guardians that the accused would re-victimize them. Other concerns expressed by the children included: fear of harassment from family members; wishing that the case had never gone to court; and extreme anger at the judge when charges were dismissed.

In five of the seven cases, the children reportedly experienced health and/or behavioural problems, which the respondents thought were related to the trauma of the court appearance. These included being depressed, anxious, unable to sleep and concentrate, having suicidal thoughts, threatening to run away, and having behavioural problems at school.

Most respondents thought the length of time it took to get to court made the process particularly difficult. Other concerns expressed were: concerns about the community finding out; the accused nonverbally intimidating the victim in court; dealing with acquittals; harshness of the defence lawyer; ongoing harassment by the accused (who in one case lived across the street); not feeling that they were being kept up-to-date on things; and a lack of coordination between the police and the child welfare workers.

When asked for their general feelings about the whole court process, six of the seven respondents were unhappy about the experience. One respondent felt generally positive about it, and stated that the outcome of the trial was just and fair, and that the professionals involved were understanding and empathic. This respondent thought the experience had a positive effect on the victim because the crown prosecutor had been very gentle and kind. In contrast, the majority of the respondents thought that the court experience had a difficult and painful impact on the victim. They thought this experience might have been improved by such things as the following: the child not having to testify in court; the child not having to look at the accused in court; the use of videotape; the child being able to sit down while testifying; having someone standing beside the child while testifying; a shorter time period between charges being laid and the case coming to court; counselling/support groups; explanation of the acquittal process; and a better understanding of what to expect from the crown prosecutors and defence lawyers.

### 5.7.7 Post Court

The only other type of assistance the families received was in the form of counselling, which members from four of the seven families received. When asked about other sources of help, respondents stated that they received most emotional support and information from other family members. Family members also provided them with accompaniment to the court proceedings. Other sources of support included agency staff, friends, an employer and a priest.

Four respondents thought the victim could have benefitted from a child victim/witness support program. Such a program, they felt, would help the child to deal with anger about the outcome and to help explain the court process. Two other respondents did not feel such a program was necessary and did not want too many people involved.

## 5.8 Summary

### 5.8.1 Perceived Problems with Substantive Sections of Bill C-15

- There was not much agreement among respondents regarding perceived problems with the substantive sections of Bill C-15.

### 5.8.2 Reported Experience with Procedural Items Related to Bill C-15

- Ban on publication (subsection 486(3)), support adults in court, and witnesses cleared from the courtroom were frequently requested by crown prosecutors, seldom objected to by defence lawyers, and were almost always allowed by judges.

- The use of videotaped evidence (section 715.1), child sitting on knee, and adult accompanying child to stand were requested some of the time by crown prosecutors, objected to frequently by defence lawyers, but usually allowed by judges.

### 5.8.3 Perceived Changes Due to Bill C-15

- There was a considerable amount of consistency among police, crown prosecutors, and judges across the study sites regarding the changes due to Bill C-15. The most common changes cited were increased reporting of child sexual abuse and more children giving evidence at younger ages.

- Defence lawyers' perceptions of the changes due to Bill C-15 were not the same as those shared by other professionals. They most frequently mentioned that there was no longer a requirement of corroboration and there was an increased use of unsworn testimony.

### 5.8.4 Impact of Testifying on the Child

- Most professionals felt that giving testimony in court was a traumatic experience for the child victim/witness. However, many also felt that the impact of testifying could be positive.

### 5.8.5 Effect of Bill C-15 on Professionals

- Most professionals felt that Bill C-15 did not change their role, but that it did increase their workload.

- Police most often reported awareness and use of special policy/protocol for dealing with child sexual abuse.

- Few professionals were aware of or received special training regarding the implementation of Bill C-15. Most, however, reported that they would participate if training were available.

### 5.8.6 Perception of Child Victim/Witnesses in Alberta

- The child victim/witness indicated that the presence of supporting family members in the courtroom helped them during testimony. Likewise, the presence of authority figures (e.g., judge and police) offered security. The presence of strangers, however, increased stress.

- The child victim/witness' feeling about the court process seemed to be directly affected by the outcome of the proceedings, i.e., victim/witnesses were more upset if the proceedings did not result in conviction.

### 5.8.7 Perception of Parents/Guardians in Alberta

- Most parents/guardians felt that the court process was generally negative and that it took too long from investigation to completion of the trial.

# 6.0 CONCLUSIONS[1]

The purpose of this report is to summarize and compare the findings of the studies conducted in Calgary and Edmonton, Alberta; Regina and Saskatoon, Saskatchewan; and Hamilton, Ontario. Three distinct study purposes were identified. All three purposes were investigated in the Alberta and Ontario studies. The Saskatchewan study, however, focussed only on the second and third purposes. The three study purposes are as follows:

(1) To explore the nature of the interrelationship between the child welfare system and the criminal justice system regarding child sexual abuse.

(2) To examine the nature of the child victim/witness experience in the criminal justice system since the proclamation of Bill C-15.

(3) To identify the degree to which the goals and objectives of Bill C-15 have been achieved.

Conclusions regarding the above study purposes are presented in this chapter. These conclusions are based on the findings that have been summarized from the site reports and are presented in Chapters 3.0, 4.0 and 5.0 of this report. The conclusions are presented below according to each specified purpose of the study.

## 6.1 The Interrelationship Between the Child Welfare System and the Criminal Justice System[2]

### 6.1.1 Protocols

Consistent with the principle of "least intrusiveness" expressed in the Alberta Child Welfare Act (1985), complete investigations of allegations of child sexual abuse are required in Calgary and Edmonton by Alberta Family and Social Services only when the alleged offender is a family member. When the alleged perpetrator is not a family member (i.e., extrafamilial abuse), and protective

---

[1] See Appendix C for a summary of the Alberta rural site study (Phillips and Hornick, 1992). The rural report findings are not comparable to the urban site studies. Therefore, a brief summary of findings is included in Appendix C.

[2] No information relevant to this section was collected in Saskatchewan.

services are determined unnecessary, the case may be referred directly to a community resource, because the child is not considered to be in need of protection.

While formal protocol in Alberta did not require inter-agency cooperation between police and Alberta Family and Social Services on all cases, there was evidence of considerable inter-agency cooperation for Calgary child sexual abuse cases when the offender lived with the child. Further, in Calgary, child welfare workers were the major source of referral of child sexual abuse cases to the police, and a considerable amount of case conferencing occurred. In Edmonton, there was even more inter-agency involvement between the police and Alberta Family and Social Services than in Calgary. The nature of the cases that were involved was also different. Calgary Social Services focussed more on intrafamilial abuse cases, whereas the data suggest that Edmonton Social Services included a considerable proportion of extrafamilial abuse cases, reflecting a broader interpretation of the Alberta Family and Social Services mandate in Edmonton. In both Calgary and Edmonton, inter-agency committees with representatives from child welfare, police, and other relevant agencies have developed protocols to guide investigations of both physical and sexual abuse.

In Hamilton, suspected incidents of child sexual abuse were reported to either the police or to a Children's Aid Society (CAS). Regardless of who first received the report, the "Child Sexual Abuse Protocol" required the police and CAS agencies to inform each other of a possible offence. Because of their legislated mandate, CAS agencies were most concerned about intrafamilial cases of child sexual abuse. However, the Catholic Children's Aid Society tended to investigate all cases of abuse.

Special Police Units

Edmonton Police Service, Calgary Police Service and the Hamilton-Wentworth Police Department all had specialized sex crime/child abuse units. In Edmonton and Hamilton, all cases of child sexual abuse were referred directly to these units. In contrast, complaints received by district offices in Calgary were often concluded by the police officer who answered the call, and were not usually referred to the special child abuse unit which is located at police headquarters.

Overlap of Cases

As might be expected due to the variations in protocol, the overlap of active case files between child welfare agencies and police in Hamilton was very high (87 percent) in comparison with Calgary (41 percent) and Edmonton (48 percent).

## 6.2 The Experiences of the Child Victim/Witness in the Criminal Justice System

### 6.2.1 Reporting Rates

Reporting of alleged occurrences of child sexual abuse to police ranged from a low of 73 per 100,000 population for Hamilton in 1990 to a high of 158 per 100,000 population in 1989 for Saskatoon. Rates for the time periods of the various studies were relatively stable, except in Saskatoon where they increased significantly from 1988 to 1990. Overall, the reporting rates of child sexual assaults are high when compared to reporting rates for all sexual assaults, i.e., adults and children. This suggests that children are significantly over represented as victims of sexual assault.

### 6.2.2 Case Profile

#### Victims

Seventy to 80 percent of the victims from all sites were female. Age distribution was also consistent, with the exception of Edmonton where victims tended to be over 12 years old. In the other sites, victims tended to be under 12 years old and a significant proportion (15 to 22 percent) were under five years old.

#### Accused

The vast majority (i.e., over 94 percent) of the accused were male and most incidents were perpetrated on a female victim. Likewise, most accused were adults, however, a significant number of accused were under 18 years old, particularly in Saskatchewan (29 percent). Overall, the majority of accused were not related to the victim. However, a significant proportion of accused (from a low of 30 percent for Saskatchewan to a high of 57 percent for Calgary) were fathers or other relatives.

#### Occurrence

Overall there was considerable consistency among the study sites in the type of abuse behaviour reported. The most common form was genital fondling, followed by oral sex. Vaginal penetration with the penis occurred in 11 percent (for Hamilton) to 20 percent (for Saskatchewan) of the cases.

## Conclusions

Overall, there is a considerable consistency among the study sites regarding case profiles. The few significant differences that do exist are likely due to differences in the protocol for recording and retaining information.

### 6.2.3 Unfounded Rates

Unfounded rates were generally low, ranging from seven percent in Edmonton to 22 percent for Hamilton cases.

## False Allegations

False allegations (i.e., victim lied) as identified by police occurred in less that five percent of the total number of cases reported to police in Hamilton and less than two percent of the total number of cases reported in Calgary.

### 6.2.4 Clearance Rates

Clearance by charge varied considerably across the study sites. Most of the variation, however, seems to be a function of record-keeping protocol and, therefore, caution should be exercised when using clearance rates as an indicator of police performance.

### 6.2.5 Conviction Rates

Conviction rates for all charges of child sexual assault were significantly high in all jurisdictions (ranging from a low of 59 percent in Edmonton to a high of 83 percent in Hamilton). Controlling for the type of court, however, indicates that Youth Court, under the Young Offenders Act, had the highest rate of conviction. Provincial Court and Court of Queen's Bench (adult accused) had lower rates of conviction.

### 6.2.6 Incarceration Rates

Overall, incarceration rates are consistent with previous research. They ranged from a low of 51 percent for Edmonton convictions to a high of 74 percent for Hamilton convictions.

### 6.2.7 Case Duration

The average time duration from occurrence, to report to police, to trial ranged from a low of eight months for Edmonton cases to a high of 11 months for Hamilton cases.

### 6.2.8 Child's Performance as a Witness

Because of the small number of cases, detailed analysis was limited to Calgary and Edmonton cases. However, the overall impressions of the court observers from all sites were very positive. They felt the child witnesses exhibited appropriate responses and coped well under stressful situations. The detailed quantitative analysis of Calgary and Edmonton court observations and the child victim/witness interviews led to the following specific conclusions.

- Children who were physically harmed during the incident had more difficulty presenting evidence.

- Children had difficulty "telling the story" if a long period of time had passed.

- The fewer strangers in the courtroom and the more supportive adults, the easier it was for the child to give evidence.

- Cross-examination by defence lawyers was significantly the most stressful part of the court process.

- Child victim/witnesses' feelings about the court process (from post court interviews) seemed to be directly affected by the outcome of the proceedings, i.e., victim/witnesses were more upset if the proceedings did not result in conviction.

## 6.3 Impact of Bill C-15

The conclusions below are presented as they pertain to the impact of specific sections of Bill C-15. In this section, our intent is to point out which components of Bill C-15 are working and which are not.

### Section 150.1 (Consent No Defence)

Consent as a defence continued to be raised by defence lawyers in Calgary (48 percent of the cases reviewed), Edmonton (18 percent) and Saskatchewan (15 percent). However, it was not raised in any of the Hamilton cases. Where consent was raised, there was no evidence regarding whether or not it was accepted by the courts. Mistaken age was very seldom raised at any of the sites. Overall, the findings suggest that section 150.1 has been successfully implemented in the study sites.

### Section 150.1(2) (Consent and Age Difference)

This section was relevant only in a small number of cases in Calgary and Edmonton. Thus, conclusions cannot be drawn on the basis of the findings.

### Section 151 (Sexual Interference)

The findings from all study sites indicate substantial use of section 151. After section 271 (Sexual assault) it was the section under which charges were most frequently laid. Further, three sites (Calgary, Edmonton and Saskatchewan) reported increasing utilization of this section over time. This increase is associated with a decrease in the use of section 271 in Calgary and Saskatchewan.

Section 151 was used to cover a broad range of conduct in all study locations. Likewise, the pattern of conduct associated with charges under section 151 was consistent among the various study sites. The most frequently reported behaviour was genital fondling, followed by other types of fondling. Less than 15 percent of the cases charged under this section involved vaginal penetration with the penis.

There was a significant tendency to lay charges under both section 151 and section 271, particularly in Calgary. Further, in both Calgary and Hamilton, a significant number of section 151 charges were withdrawn. This could be an indication of plea negotiation or, alternatively, some crown prosecutors may have preferred to proceed under the more tested section 271.

Conviction rates for section 151 were high in all jurisdictions, ranging from 52 percent to 80 percent. The high conviction rates, however, were due to a large extent to a high rate of guilty pleas, particularly in Edmonton and Saskatchewan, and high rates of charges withdrawn in Hamilton and Calgary. For those convicted, incarceration rates were 48 percent in Edmonton and 60 percent in Calgary. Further, the most common incarceration time in Calgary was low, with

50 percent receiving a sentence of three months or less, compared to 30 percent of the Edmonton cases receiving a sentence of three months or less.

The extensive use of section 151, the high conviction rates, and the application of the section to a broad range of behaviour all lead to the conclusion that section 151 has been fully implemented and is an appropriate, effective section.

Section 152 (Sexual Invitation)

While significantly fewer charges were reported under section 152 than section 151, this would be expected given the more specific application of this section. On the basis of limited data, however, it was used to cover a broad range of conduct including invitation to touch and exposure, which are less intrusive conducts than those covered by section 151. Conviction rates were also significantly high. Overall, section 152 seems to be a useful and effective section, although it is by definition limited to certain types of conduct.

Section 153 (Sexual Exploitation)

In all locations, few charges were reported under section 153. The fact that this charge is aimed at protection of the older victim (i.e., 15 to 18 years old) and, as well, is limited to accused who are in a position of authority or trust, may account for its limited application.

Despite the lack of application, an assessment of section 153, as well as sections 151 and 152, should not be conducted in isolation from the other sections. They are in reality a "set" of specific charges designed to cover a total range of situations, with section 151 being the broadest and section 153 being the most specific.

Female Offenders (Sections 151, 152 and 153)

The small number of cases involving female offenders which went to disposition was somewhat unexpected since five percent of the cases investigated by police in Calgary and two percent of the cases investigated in Edmonton involved female suspects. However, most of these cases seem to be screened out prior to laying charges. If we consider only cases where the police have cleared by charge, this proportion drops to less than two percent (n=6) in Calgary and (n=9) in Edmonton.

Section 155 (Incest); Section 159 (Anal Intercourse); Section 160 (Bestiality); Section 170 (Parent/Guardian Procuring); Section 171 (Householder Permitting Sexual Activity); Section 172 (Corrupting Children)

The frequency of these offences was too low for any meaningful analysis. Either the conduct covered by these sections seldom occurs (as the data from these studies imply), or they are too difficult to enforce.

Subsection 173(2) (Exposure to Children Under 14 years of Age)

Use of subsection 173(2) was infrequently reported. Calgary police, for example, laid only two charges under this section during the study. In Edmonton, where the section was most frequently used, charges were laid under this section when exposure was the only behaviour that occurred. When exposure occurred with other more serious behaviour, which it often did, police tended to lay charges under the more serious hybrid and indictable offence, and did not bother using this summary offence. Thus, although few charges were laid under this section and conviction tended to occur through guilty pleas (particularly in Edmonton), section 173(2) does seem to be useful for the "exposure only" summary offences.

Subsections 212(2) and (4) (Living On The Avails and Obtaining for Sexual Purpose Persons Under 18 Years Old)

During 1989, nine charges were laid under section 212 in Calgary. In 1990, the number decreased to five charges. In Edmonton, ten charges were laid under section 212 in 1989 and five in 1990. In Saskatchewan, only seven charges were laid under these sections and no charges were laid in Hamilton.

The number of charges under section 212 do not seem to reflect the real level of the problem of juvenile prostitution. The Calgary Police Commission Prostitution Report (1991) provides a probable explanation. This report documents that in 1988, 52 charges were laid under section 195.1 (Soliciting) against female prostitutes under 18 years old. In 1989, there were 57 charges under section 195.1 and this rose to 79 charges in 1990. The age of the female prostitute charged under this section was as low as 13 years old. Unfortunately, comparable data were not available for any of the other sites. However, it is reasonable to assume that the trend of using section 195.1 to deal with female prostitution under 18 years of age would also hold.

The lack of use of subsections 212(2) and (4) and the continued use of section 195.1 is not consistent with the spirit of Bill C-15, i.e., the protection of the young. However, the objective of the use of section 195.1, according to the Calgary Police report, was to prevent the young person continuing to work as a prostitute (Calgary Police Commission Prostitution Report, 1991). With the help of the Justice of the Peace and the youth court judges, the youth have often been barred from the "stroll" areas of Calgary as a condition of release. Thus, the police seem to be applying the solicitation legislation simply because it is easier to enforce.

Further, anecdotal information obtained during the study and data from the professional survey suggest that subsection 212(2) (Living on the avails) is only enforceable when a prostitute "turns" against a pimp. Likewise, charges under subsection 212(4) (Obtaining a person under 18 years of age for sexual purposes) could only be enforced if the "John" was caught in the act. Thus, traditional policing methods do not seem to be appropriate for enforcement of subsections 212(2) and (4). Therefore, these sections have not been effective in dealing with the problem of juvenile prostitution.

### Section 271 (Sexual Assault)

As indicated in the discussion of section 151, section 271 is often used in combination with section 151. The impact of the use of section 271 in this study was impressive. The conviction rate was very high in all locations. Further, guilty pleas were high and rates of charges withdrawn were relatively low. The incarceration rates were also high. Overall, the results of the site studies indicate that section 271 is being used quite effectively to deal with child sexual assault in the criminal justice system.

### Section 272 (Sexual Assault, Level II, Sexual Assault, Level III)

The low frequency of these charges prohibits analysis.

### Section 274 (Corroboration Not Required)

Such variables as the presence of more than one victim and the presence of a corroborative witness appeared to be important predictors in the decision by police to lay charges. However, they were not significant predictors of conviction at trial. This finding, along with the absence of any indication of concern regarding corroboration seems to support the interpretation that the courts are considering section 274 seriously since a considerable number of cases resulted in conviction without any type of corroboration.

### Section 275 (Recent Complaint Abrogated)

In the past, courts were permitted to allow into evidence statements made to a third party by the victim of a sexual assault. Section 275 abrogating this rule of recent complaint in sexual offences, which was first enacted in 1982 (Bill C-127), was extended to the new Bill C-15 sexual offences. No data were directly relevant to the abrogation of recent complaint.

Subsection 276(1) (Sexual Activity)

Past sexual activities were very seldom raised as a defence in proceedings at any of the study sites. Thus, the absence of data to the contrary would suggest that this section has been implemented and was effective in child sexual abuse cases. This section, however, was struck down by the Supreme Court of Canada in August 1991 in R. v. Seaboyer; R. v. Gayme.

Section 277 (Reputation Evidence)

Reputation was never raised by defence in the cases studied in Calgary and Hamilton. However, it was raised in 18 percent of the Edmonton cases and four percent of the Saskatchewan cases. Perhaps the relative older age of the victims in Edmonton may account for the frequency at that location. The absence and relatively low occurrence of questions in proceedings concerning reputation evidence suggests that this section has also been relatively effective.

Subsection 486(2.1) (Testimony Outside the Courtroom)

There was considerable variation among the study sites in relation to the implementation of subsection 486(2.1). For example, the screen was used in one-quarter of the cases observed in Saskatchewan, as well as nine percent of the cases in the Calgary courts. Hamilton courts, however, seldom used the screen at all. Saskatchewan courts were the only courts that used closed-circuit television (24 percent) during the time period of the study. The only other innovation used in a significant number of cases at all locations was support adults staying in the court. These data indicate that there are major problems with the adoption and implementation of this component of Bill C-15. Other innovations, however, were used.

Subsection 486(3) (Order Restricting Publication)

Requests for a ban on publication were made in over 50 of the cases and were almost always ordered. Although this section predates Bill C-15, it is particularly relevant to sexual assault cases and is being used.

### Section 715.1 (Videotaped Evidence)

During the time period of the study, videotapes of the victim were made for 34 percent of the Saskatchewan cases, 18 percent of the Edmonton cases, three Calgary cases, and none of the Hamilton cases. Because of the R. v. Thompson (1989) judgement in Alberta, very few videotapes were actually used in court proceedings. While the R. v. Thompson judgement essentially blocked the implementation of this component of Bill C-15, it is interesting to note that Edmonton and Saskatchewan police continued to use videotaping as an investigative tool.

### Subsection 16(3) Canada Evidence Act (Oath)

Over three-quarters of the child victim/witnesses in Calgary and one-half of the child victim/witnesses in Edmonton were sworn. The rest gave testimony under the promise to tell the truth provision. In Hamilton, four of five child victim/witnesses were sworn. This provision seems to have been readily implemented and thus is facilitating children giving evidence.

### Additional Issue: Time Limitation

Prior to Bill C-15, section 141 provided that certain enumerated sexual offences could not be prosecuted if more than one year had elapsed from the time the alleged offence had occurred. This limitation was repealed by Bill C-15.

The repeal of this limitation period was meant to protect children in situations where disclosure was delayed. For a small number of cases in this study, (i.e., six percent of the relevant cases in Calgary and two percent in Edmonton), disclosure was made more than one year after the incident, and resulted in a 60 percent conviction rate in Calgary. A very high number of the relevant charges (77 percent) were also withdrawn in Calgary. However, problems prosecuting such cases could be due to difficulties the child might have had in remembering details of the offences.

## 6.4 Achievement of the Goals

As discussed in Chapter 1.0 of this report, the amendments to the Criminal Code outlined in Bill C-15 were driven by four broad policy goals. The level to which these goals has been achieved reflects not only on the relative success of components of Bill C-15, but also on the appropriateness of the policy behind the bill. Therefore, the goals are reviewed below in light of the overall findings of the site studies.

### 6.4.1 Goal # 1: To Provide Better Protection to Child Sexual Abuse Victim/Witnesses

The findings of this report strongly support the conclusion that the amendments outlined in Bill C-15 have provided better protection to child sexual abuse victim/witnesses. The specific findings which support this conclusion are listed below.

- There was a high degree of inter-agency cooperation in the development of protocols for dealing with child sexual abuse both in Ontario and Alberta.

- Calgary and Edmonton, Alberta, and Hamilton, Ontario police all had special child abuse investigation units.

- Reporting of alleged occurrences of child sexual abuse was high in all jurisdictions, ranging from a low of 73 per 100,000 in 1990 in Hamilton to a high of 158 per 100,000 in 1989 in Saskatoon.

- Children are significantly over represented as victims of sexual assault.

- Most victims were female under 12 years old and a significant number were under five years old (15 to 22 percent).

- A significant number (17 to 29 percent) of the accused were young offenders (12 to 17 years old).

- The number of charges under sections of Bill C-15 was high and increased over time. The number of charges laid under section 271 (Sexual assault) was also high.

- Conviction rates for most sections were high, especially if the accused was a young offender.

- Guilty plea rates were high, especially for section 271 (Sexual assault).

- A broad range of conduct was covered by section 151 (Sexual interference), section 152 (Sexual touching), section 153 (Sexual exploitation), and section 271 (Sexual assault).

- Many cases (20 to 30 percent) involve male victims and some female offenders were charged.

In addition to the above supportive findings, the following issues were identified:

- The lack of charges under subsection 212(2) (Living on the avails) and subsection 212(4) (Obtaining for sexual purposes) indicate that juvenile prostitutes were not helped by the new legislation.

- A significant proportion of substantiated cases did not conclude with charges being laid and subsequent conviction. Little is known about these cases. Further, if the cases involved an accused not related to the victim, the victim tended not to be followed up by the child welfare system.

### 6.4.2 Goal # 2: To Enhance Successful Prosecution of Child Sexual Abuse Cases

The findings of this report generally support the conclusion that Bill C-15 procedural amendments have enhanced prosecution of child sexual abuse cases. The findings supporting this conclusion are listed below.

- In court proceedings, the child victim/witness was usually sworn, especially if they were over 12 years of age.

- If the child was not sworn, evidence was always taken under the promise to tell the truth.

- Corroboration was important for laying charges, but was not found to be related to conviction in trial.

- Some expert witnesses were being used, especially with younger children.

- Videotaping was found to be useful for police investigations and refreshing the child's memory prior to proceedings, as was the case in
R. v. Beauchamp and Beauchamp.

The nonsupporting findings were as follows:

- R. v. Thompson limited the use of videotapes as evidence during the time of the site studies.

### 6.4.3 Goal # 3: To Improve the Experience of the Child Victim/Witness

Assuming that all appearances in court as a victim of sexual assault are traumatic (whether the victim is an adult or a child), the findings of the site studies suggest that the changes due to Bill C-15, as well as other innovations, have improved the experience of the child victim/witness within the criminal justice system. The following findings led us to this conclusion.

- Ban on publication (subsection 486(3)) was widely used in all jurisdictions.

- The child victim/witness was usually allowed to turn away from the accused. In some jurisdictions, this was facilitated by the layout of the courtroom.

- Support adults were often present during court proceedings, and it was found that their presence made it easier for the child to give evidence.

- There is an openness on the part of judges, crown prosecutors, and defence lawyers to use innovative supports for children who are giving evidence.

In addition to the above supportive findings, a number of issues were identified and are listed below.

- Screens and closed-circuit television were seldom used.

- In the few cases where videotapes were used for evidence, the child was still extensively cross-examined.

- Children had difficulty "telling the story" if a long period of time had passed since the incident.

- Cross-examination by defence lawyers was significantly the most stressful part of the court process for the child victim/witness.

### 6.4.4 Goal # 4: To Bring Sentencing in Line with the Severity of the Offence

Unfortunately, sufficient data are not available to make any conclusions regarding this goal. Comparison and trend data are needed to reflect on the issue of adequacy of sentencing. The few relevant findings available are listed below.

- Incarceration rates for section 151 (Sexual interference) and section 271 (Sexual assault) ranged from 48 percent (for section 151 in Edmonton) to a high of 62 percent (for section 271 in Calgary).

- Time of incarceration for section 271 was slightly higher than for section 151 (section 151 = 6.7 months in Calgary and 11.1 months in Edmonton compared to section 271 = 9.9 months in Calgary and 11.2 months in Edmonton).

## 6.5 Overview

An overview of the impact of Bill C-15 can be summarized as follows:

- The substantive components of Bill C-15 are providing better protection to children who have been sexually abused.

- The procedural components of Bill C-15 are contributing to successful prosecution of child sexual abuse cases.

- The use of innovations during court proceedings improves the experience of the child victim/witness.

We are confident in concluding that most aspects of Bill C-15 are working well, and that the professionals involved have adapted to and accepted the changes. We wish to stress, however, as our data indicate, the scope and complex nature of the problem of child sexual abuse requires a response far broader than a legal response alone.

# APPENDIX A

# MAJOR RESEARCH EVALUATION REPORTS ON CHILD SEXUAL ABUSE AND THE IMPACT OF BILL C-15

# MAJOR RESEARCH EVALUATION REPORTS ON CHILD SEXUAL ABUSE AND THE IMPACT OF BILL C-15

### Calgary and Edmonton, Alberta

Hornick, J.P., Burrows, B., Perry, D., and Bolitho, F. (1992). <u>Review and Monitoring of Child Sexual Abuse Cases in Selected Sites in Alberta</u>. Prepared for Justice Canada and Health and Welfare Canada by the Canadian Research Institute for Law and the Family.

### Rural Alberta

Phillips, D., and Hornick, J.P. (1992). <u>Review and Monitoring of Child Sexual Abuse Cases in Selected Sites in Rural Alberta</u>. Prepared for Justice Canada and Health and Welfare Canada by the Canadian Research Institute for Law and the Family.

### Hamilton, Ontario

Campbell Research Associates and Social Data Research Ltd., (1992). <u>Review and Monitoring of Child Sexual Abuse Cases in Selected Sites in Hamilton-Wentworth, Ontario</u>. Prepared for Justice Canada.

### Regina and Saskatoon, Saskatchewan

Fischer, D.G., Stevens, G., and Berg, L. (1992). <u>Review and Monitoring of Child Sexual Abuse Cases in Selected Sites in Saskatchewan</u>. Prepared for Justice Canada by Peat Marwick Stevenson & Kellogg, Management Consultants.

# APPENDIX B

# TABLES AND FIGURES

# LIST OF TABLES

| Table B-1 | Return Rates of Child Sexual Abuse Questionnaires by Profession and Location | 127 |
|---|---|---|
| Table B-2 | Reliability of Subscales Developed for the Court Observation Rating Scale | 128 |
| Table B-3 | List of Variables of Knowledge Seeker Analysis for Decision to Lay Charges | 129 |
| Table B-4 | List of Sample Parameters and Variables of Knowledge Seeker Analysis | 130 |
| Table B-5 | Number of Charges Under Sections Relevant to Child Sexual Abuse and Assault in Calgary from 1986 -1990 | 131 |
| Table B-6 | Number of Charges Under Sections Relevant to Child Sexual Abuse and Assault in Edmonton from 1986 - 1990 | 132 |
| Table B-7 | Number of Charges under Sections Relevant to Child Sexual Abuse and Assault During the Period 1988 - 1990 | 133 |
| Table B-8 | Experience with Procedural Items for Crown Prosecutors by Location | 134 |
| Table B-9 | Experience with Procedural Items for Defence Lawyers by Location | 135 |
| Table B-10 | Experience with Procedural Items for Judges by Location | 136 |

# LIST OF FIGURES

Figure B-1  Prediction Model for Witness Behaviour: Anxious/Withdrawn for Calgary Court Proceedings . . . . . . . . . . . . . . . . . . . . . . . 137

Figure B-2  Prediction Model for Witness Behaviour: Ability to Communicate for Calgary Court Proceedings . . . . . . . . . . . . . . . . . . . . . . . 138

Figure B-3  Prediction Model for Witness Behaviour: Anxious/Withdrawn for Edmonton Court Proceedings . . . . . . . . . . . . . . . . . . . . . . . 139

Figure B-4  Prediction Model for Witness Behaviour: Sad/Cries for Edmonton Court Proceedings . . . . . . . . . . . . . . . . . . . . . . . 140

Figure B-5  Prediction Model for Witness Behaviour: Ability to Communicate for Edmonton Court Proceedings . . . . . . . . . . . . . . . . . . . . . . . 141

### Table B-1  Return Rates of Child Sexual Abuse Questionnaires by Profession and Location

|  | Judges | | Crown Prosecutors | | Defence Counsel | | Police | | Child Welfare Workers | |
|---|---|---|---|---|---|---|---|---|---|---|
|  | n | % | n | % | n | % | n | % | n | % |
| Calgary and Edmonton Return Rate | 40 | 34.0 | 52 | 55.0 | 46 | 46.0 | 63 | 78.0 | 135 | 48.0 |
| Hamilton Return Rate | 7 | 41.0 | 6 | 46.0 | 3 | 14.0 | 6 | 43.0 | 12 | 40.0 |
| Saskatchewan Return Rate | 22 | 28.0 | 17 | 63.0 | 10 | 20.0 | 24 | 86.0 | N/A | |

**Table B-2** **Reliability of Subscales Developed for the Court Observation Rating Scale[1]**

| Subscale and Component Items | Reliability Coefficient[2] |
|---|---|
| Anxious/Withdrawn<br><br>　Fidgets<br>　Anxious<br>　Withdrawn<br>　Worried<br>　Shy/Timid<br>　Appears Confused | .8190 |
| Sad/Cries<br><br>　Sad<br>　Cries<br>　Easily Embarassed | .6808 |
| Able to Communicate<br><br>　Child's Speech - How Fluent?<br>　Child's Speech - How Audible?<br>　Detail Child Spontaneously Provided<br>　Degree of Confidence While Testifying | .8115 |

---

[1] Factor analysis was used to develop subscales from the original items.

[2] Cronbach's Alpha.

**Table B-3    List of Variables of Knowledge Seeker Analysis for Decision to Lay Charges**

| Location | Calgary and Edmonton | |
|---|---|---|
| | | Range |
| Independent Variables | 1) Person child disclosed to<br>2) Family resistance<br>3) When occurrence was reported<br>4) Who reported<br>5) Number of victims<br>6) Number of offenders[1]<br>7) Gender of victim<br>8) Age of victim when reported<br>9) Duration of abuse[1]<br>10) Gender of offender[1]<br>11) Age when abuse began<br>12) Relationship of offender to victim<br>13) Level of intrusion<br>14) Used force[1]<br>15) Use of enticement<br>16) Use of alcohol[1]<br>17) Use of drugs[1]<br>18) Witness<br>19) Physical injuries<br>20) Emotional injury<br>21) Forensic examination<br>22) First agency contact[1]<br>23) Age of offender | 1 - 12<br>1 - 2<br>1 - 6<br>1 - 16<br>1 - 2<br>1 - 2<br>1 - 2<br>1 - 6<br>1 - 6<br>1 - 2<br>1 - 6<br>1 - 16<br>1 - 13<br>1 - 3<br>1 - 2<br>1 - 2<br>1 - 2<br>1 - 2<br>1 - 2<br>1 - 2<br>1 - 2<br>1 - 6<br>1 - 8 |
| Dependent Variable | Charged and Other Cases[2] | |

---

[1] These variables were not included in the analysis of the Hamilton data.

[2] Unfounded cases, cases where the alleged offender is under 12 years of age and cannot be charged, and cases where the offender is unknown have been omitted from this analysis.

**Table B-4    List of Sample Parameters and Variables of Knowledge Seeker Analysis**

| | Variables | |
|---|---|---|
| Independent Variables | | <u>Range</u> |
| | 1)  Gender of witness | 1 - 2 |
| | 2)  Age of witness | 1 - 6 |
| | 3)  Total time of examination-in-chief | 1 - 9 |
| | 4)  Total time of cross-examination | 1 - 9 |
| | 5)  Number of court appearances | 1 - 4 |
| | 6)  Number of victims | 1 - 2 |
| | 7)  Number of alleged offenders | 1 - 2 |
| | 8)  Gender of alleged offenders | 1 - 2 |
| | 9)  Use of weapon | 1 - 2 |
| | 10) Number of witnesses | 1 - 3 |
| | 11) Expert witnesses | 1 - 2 |
| | 12) Person child disclosed to | 1 - 12 |
| | 13) When occurrence was reported | 1 - 6 |
| | 14) Who reported | 1 - 16 |
| | 15) Relationship of offender to victim | 1 - 16 |
| | 16) Level of intrusion of abuse | 1 - 13 |
| | 17) Use of force | 1 - 3 |
| | 18) Use of enticement | 1 - 2 |
| | 19) Use of alcohol | 1 - 2 |
| | 20) Use of drugs | 1 - 2 |
| | 21) Physical injuries | 1 - 2 |
| | 22) Emotional injury | 1 - 2 |
| | 23) Forensic examination | 1 - 2 |
| | 24) First agency contact | 1 - 6 |
| | 25) Age of alleged offender | 1 - 8 |
| | 26) Duration of abuse | 1 - 6 |
| | 27) Innovative procedures used | 1 - 3 |
| | 28) Number of people in courtroom during child witness testimony | 1 - 7 |
| | 29) Support adult stays in courtroom | 1 - 2 |
| | 30) Witnesses cleared from court | 1 - 2 |
| Dependent Variables | Witness behaviour: Anxious/Withdrawn; Sad/Cries; Ability to Communicate | |

## Table B-5  Number of Charges Under Sections Relevant to Child Sexual Abuse and Assault in Calgary from 1986 -1990

| Charge Section Number[1] | 1986 n | 1986 % | 1987 n | 1987 % | 1988 n | 1988 % | 1989 n | 1989 % | 1990 n | 1990 % |
|---|---|---|---|---|---|---|---|---|---|---|
| **Old Code XCC** | | | | | | | | | | |
| Sections 146(1) & (2) | 5 | 3.2 | 6 | 2.8 | | | | | | |
| Section 150 | 3 | 1.9 | 2 | 0.9 | | | | | | |
| Section 151 | | | | | | | | | | |
| Section 152 | 1 | 0.6 | | | | | | | | |
| Section 153 | | | | | | | | | | |
| Section 155 | 2 | 1.3 | 1 | 0.5 | | | | | | |
| Section 156 | | | | | | | | | | |
| Section 157 | 30 | 19.5 | 55 | 25.7 | | | | | | |
| Section 166 | | | | | | | | | | |
| Section 167 | | | | | | | | | | |
| Section 168 | | | | | | | | | | |
| Section 169 | 11 | 7.1 | 12 | 5.6 | | | | | | |
| **Sexual Assault Old/New Code[2]** | | | | | | | | | | |
| Sections 246.1, 246.2, 246.3[3] and Section 271 | 102 | 66.2 | 138 | 64.5 | 147 | 57.2 | 156 | 49.7 | 130 | 46.8 |
| Section 272 | | | | | | | 8 | 2.5 | 6 | 2.2 |
| Section 273 | | | | | | | | | | |
| **New Code** | | | | | | | | | | |
| Section 151 | | | | | 47 | 18.3 | 81 | 25.8 | 74 | 26.6 |
| Section 152 | | | | | 9 | 3.5 | 6 | 1.9 | 14 | 5.0 |
| Section 153 | | | | | 5 | 1.9 | 15 | 4.8 | 17 | 6.1 |
| Section 155 | | | | | 5 | 1.9 | 3 | 1.0 | 5 | 1.8 |
| Section 159 | | | | | 2 | 0.8 | 8 | 2.5 | 2 | 0.7 |
| Section 160 | | | | | | | | | | |
| Section 170 | | | | | | | | | | |
| Section 171 | | | | | | | | | | |
| Section 172 | | | | | | | | | | |
| Sections 173(1) & (2) | | | | | 42 | 16.3 | 28 | 8.9 | 25 | 9.0 |
| Section 212 | | | | | | | 9 | 2.9 | 5 | 1.8 |
| **TOTALS** | 154 | 100.0 | 214 | 100.0 | 257 | 100.0 | 314 | 100.0 | 278 | 100.0 |
| Percentage change over previous year | | | | + 39.0% | | + 20.1% | | + 22.2% | | - 11.5% |

Data Source: Police Information Management System (PIMS)
Unit of Analysis: Charge

[1] See Table 1.1, pages 5-6, for a brief description of each section.

[2] The new <u>Criminal Code</u> was proclaimed January 1, 1988. Sexual assault sections 246.1, 246.2 and 246.3 were changed to sections 271, 272 and 273 respectively, however, the contents of these sections were not changed.

[3] Distinctions are not made on most code subsections (e.g., section 246.1 v. section 246.2) since the Police Information System captures only 3 digits.

## Table B-6  Number of Charges Under Sections Relevant to Child Sexual Abuse and Assault in Edmonton from 1986 - 1990

| Charge Section Number[1] | 1986 n | 1986 % | 1987 n | 1987 % | 1988 n | 1988 % | 1989 n | 1989 % | 1990 n | 1990 % |
|---|---|---|---|---|---|---|---|---|---|---|
| **Old Code XCC** | | | | | | | | | | |
| Sections 146(1) & (2) | 15 | 5.7 | 8 | 3.6 | 10 | 3.8 | 1 | 0.4 | 7 | 2.0 |
| Section 150 | 6 | 2.3 | 4 | 1.8 | | | | | | |
| Section 151 | | | | | | | | | | |
| Section 152 | | | | | | | | | | |
| Section 153 | | | | | | | | | | |
| Section 155 | 6 | 2.3 | 3 | 1.3 | 3 | 1.1 | 3 | 1.1 | 1 | 0.3 |
| Section 156 | | | | | 2 | 0.8 | | | | |
| Section 157 | 28 | 10.7 | 31 | 13.8 | 20 | 7.5 | 9 | 3.2 | 16 | 4.5 |
| Section 166 | | | | | | | | | | |
| Section 167 | | | | | | | | | | |
| Section 168 | | | | | | | | | | |
| Section 169 | 27 | 10.3 | 15 | 6.7 | | | | | | |
| **Sexual Assault Old/New Code[2]** | | | | | | | | | | |
| Sections 246.1, 246.2 & 246.3[3] and Section 271 | 176 | 67.4 | 160 | 71.4 | 164 | 61.7 | 159 | 56.4 | 191 | 53.4 |
| Section 272 | 3 | 1.1 | 2 | 0.9 | 4 | 1.5 | 5 | 1.8 | | |
| Section 273 | | | 1 | 0.4 | | | 1 | 0.4 | | |
| **New Code** | | | | | | | | | | |
| Section 151 | | | | | 19 | 7.1 | 45 | 16.0 | 76 | 21.2 |
| Section 152 | | | | | 11 | 4.1 | 9 | 3.2 | 13 | 3.6 |
| Section 153 | | | | | 2 | 0.8 | 8 | 2.8 | 6 | 1.7 |
| Section 155 | | | | | 7 | 2.6 | 1 | 0.4 | 6 | 1.7 |
| Section 159 | | | | | 3 | 1.1 | 2 | 0.7 | 4 | 1.1 |
| Section 160 | | | | | | | | | 3 | 0.8 |
| Section 170 | | | | | | | | | | |
| Section 171 | | | | | | | | | | |
| Section 172 | | | | | | | | | | |
| Section 173(1) | | | | | 14 | 5.3 | 24 | 8.5 | 23 | 6.4 |
| Section 173(2) | | | | | 6 | 2.3 | 5 | 1.8 | 7 | 2.0 |
| Section 212 | | | | | 1 | 0.4 | 10 | 3.5 | 5 | 1.4 |
| **TOTALS** | 261 | 100.0 | 224 | 100.0 | 266 | 100.0 | 282 | 100.0 | 358 | 100.0 |
| Percentage change over previous year | | | -14.2% | | +18.8% | | +6.0% | | +27.0% | |

Data Source: Police Information Systems (Records and CIA)
Unit of Analysis: Charge

[1] See Table 1.1, pages 5-6, for a brief description of each section.

[2] The new <u>Criminal Code</u> was proclaimed January 1, 1988. Sexual assault sections 246.1, 246.1 and 246.3 were changed to sections 271, 272 and 273 respectively, however, the contents of these sections were not changed.

[3] Distinctions are not made on most code subsections (e.g., section 246.1 v. section 246.2) since the Police Information System captures only 3 digits.

## Table B-7   Number of Charges under Sections Relevant to Child Sexual Abuse and Assault During the Period 1988 - 1990[1]

| Section Number | 1988 n | 1988 % | 1989 n | 1989 % | 1990 n | 1990 % |
|---|---|---|---|---|---|---|
| **Old Code:** | | | | | | |
| Section 140 | 17 | 2.2 | 4 | 0.5 | 2 | 0.3 |
| Section 141 | 1 | 0.1 | | | | |
| Section 146(1)(2) | 5 | 0.6 | 3 | 0.3 | | |
| Section 149 | 3 | 0.4 | 6 | 0.8 | 2 | 0.3 |
| Section 150 | | | 2 | 0.3 | | |
| Section 151 | | | 2 | 0.3 | 7 | 0.9 |
| Section 152 | | | | | 1 | 0.1 |
| Section 153 | | | 2 | 0.3 | 3 | 0.3 |
| Section 156 | | | | | 4 | 0.5 |
| Section 157 | 4 | 0.5 | 6 | 0.8 | | |
| Section 169 | 5 | 0.6 | | | | |
| **Sexual Assault Old/New Code:** | | | | | | |
| Section 195 | | | 4 | 0.5 | | |
| Section 246(1) | 110 | 14.0 | 90 | 11.5 | 12 | 1.5 |
| Section 246(2) | 3 | 0.4 | 3 | 0.4 | | |
| Section 247 | 4 | 0.5 | | | | |
| Section 271 | 2 | 0.3 | 134 | 17.1 | 69 | 8.8 |
| Section 272 | | | 2 | 0.3 | 1 | 0.1 |
| **New Code:** | | | | | | |
| Section 151 | 1 | 0.1 | 68 | 8.7 | 137 | 17.5 |
| Section 152 | 1 | 0.1 | 10 | 1.3 | 2 | 0.2 |
| Section 153 | | | 6 | 0.8 | 10 | 1.3 |
| Section 155 | | | 1 | 0.1 | 4 | 0.5 |
| Section 159 | | | 2 | 0.3 | 5 | 0.6 |
| Section 173(2) | | | 2 | 0.3 | 12 | 1.5 |
| Section 212 | | | 7 | 0.9 | | |
| Section 279 | | | | | 4 | 0.5 |
| **TOTALS** | 156 | 19.9 | 354 | 45.1 | 275 | 35.0 |
| Percentage change over previous year | | | + 127% | | - 22% | |

[1] Data Source: Police File Review
Unit of Analysis: Charge
Missing = 11

## Table B-8   Experience with Procedural Items for Crown Prosecutors by Location

| Item Requested | CALGARY (n=35) | | | | | | HAMILTON (n=6) | | | | | | SASKATOON (n=17) | | | | | |
|---|---|---|---|---|---|---|---|---|---|---|---|---|---|---|---|---|---|---|
| | Requested n | % | Objecting n | % | Allowed n | % | Requested n | % | Objecting n | % | Allowed n | % | Requested n | % | Objecting n | % | Allowed n | % |
| Videotape (s.715.1)* | 13 | 37.1 | 11 | 84.6 | 10 | 76.9 | - | - | - | - | - | - | 7 | 41.2 | - | - | - | - |
| Screens (s.486(2.1))* | 17 | 48.6 | 9 | 52.9 | 10 | 58.8 | 2 | 33.0 | 1 | 50.0 | 1 | 50.0 | 10 | 58.8 | - | - | - | - |
| Booster Seat | 14 | 40.0 | - | - | 9 | 64.3 | 1 | 17.0 | 1 | 100.0 | 1 | 100.0 | 2 | 11.8 | - | - | - | - |
| Child Brings Toy | 13 | 37.1 | - | - | 11 | 84.6 | 1 | 17.0 | - | - | 1 | 100.0 | 1 | 5.9 | - | - | - | - |
| Child Sits on Knee | 8 | 22.9 | 7 | 87.5 | 4 | 50.0 | - | - | - | - | - | - | 5 | 29.4 | 5 | 100.0 | 3 | 60.0 |
| Adult Accompanied to Stand | 18 | 51.4 | 11 | 61.1 | 13 | 72.2 | 2 | 33.0 | 2 | 100.0 | 1 | 50.0 | 13 | 76.5 | 7 | 53.9 | 12 | 92.3 |
| Support Adult in Court | 33 | 94.3 | 12 | 36.4 | 25 | 75.8 | 5 | 83.0 | 2 | 40.0 | 4 | 80.0 | 14 | 82.4 | 7 | 50.0 | 13 | 92.9 |
| Witnesses Cleared | 33 | 94.3 | 12 | 36.4 | 25 | 75.8 | 4 | 67.0 | 1 | 25.0 | 4 | 100.0 | 11 | 64.7 | 7 | 63.6 | 9 | 81.8 |
| Spectators Cleared | 32 | 91.4 | 19 | 59.4 | 26 | 81.3 | 4 | 67.0 | 1 | 25.0 | 4 | 100.0 | 11 | 64.7 | 7 | 63.6 | 9 | 81.8 |
| Ban on Publication (s.486(3))* | 35 | 100.0 | 9 | 25.7 | 29 | 82.9 | 6 | 100.0 | - | - | 5 | 83.0 | 7 | 41.2 | 2 | 28.6 | 5 | 71.4 |
| Child Testifies Turned Away | 9 | 25.7 | 2 | 22.2 | 7 | 77.8 | - | - | - | - | - | - | 5 | 29.4 | 2 | 40.0 | 5 | 100.0 |
| Microphone | - | - | - | - | - | - | - | - | - | - | - | - | 10 | 58.8 | - | - | - | - |
| Props | - | - | - | - | - | - | - | - | - | - | - | - | 10 | 58.8 | - | - | - | - |
| Expert as Interpreter | 1 | 2.9 | 1 | 100.0 | 1 | 100.0 | - | - | - | - | - | - | - | - | - | - | - | - |
| Expert Testifies re Child's Testimony. | 14 | 40.0 | 8 | 57.1 | 13 | 92.9 | 1 | 17.0 | - | - | 1 | 100.0 | 4 | 23.5 | - | - | - | - |

* These procedural items are part of Bill C-15.

**Table B-9    Experience with Procedural Items for Defence Lawyers by Location**

| Item Requested | CALGARY (n=24) | | | | | | HAMILTON (n=3) | | | | | | SASKATOON (n=10) | | | | | |
|---|---|---|---|---|---|---|---|---|---|---|---|---|---|---|---|---|---|---|
| | Requested n | % | Objecting n | % | Allowed n | % | Requested n | % | Objecting n | % | Allowed n | % | Requested n | % | Objecting n | % | Allowed n | % |
| Videotape (s.715.1)* | 3 | 12.5 | 2 | 66.7 | 3 | 100.0 | - | - | - | - | - | - | 6 | 60.0 | 3 | 50.0 | 5 | 83.3 |
| Screens (s.486(2.1))* | 7 | 29.2 | 4 | 57.1 | 5 | 71.4 | - | - | - | - | - | - | 6 | 60.0 | - | - | - | - |
| Booster Seat | 1 | 4.2 | - | - | 1 | 100.0 | 1 | 33.0 | - | - | 1 | 100.0 | 1 | 10.0 | - | - | - | - |
| Child Brings Toy | 1 | 4.2 | - | - | 1 | 100.0 | - | - | - | - | - | - | 1 | 10.0 | 1 | 100.0 | 1 | 100.0 |
| Child Sits on Knee | - | - | - | - | - | - | - | - | - | - | - | - | 1 | 20.0 | - | - | - | - |
| Adult Accompanied to Stand | 4 | 16.7 | 2 | 50.0 | 2 | 50.0 | 1 | 33.0 | 1 | 100.0 | - | - | 1 | 10.0 | - | - | - | - |
| Support Adult in Court | 16 | 66.7 | 2 | 12.5 | 14 | 87.5 | 3 | 100.0 | 1 | 33.0 | 1 | 33.0 | 8 | 80.0 | 1 | 2.5 | 4 | 50.0 |
| Witnesses Cleared | 17 | 70.8 | 2 | 11.8 | 14 | 82.3 | 1 | 33.0 | - | - | 1 | 100.0 | 7 | 70.0 | 1 | 14.3 | 4 | 57.1 |
| Spectators Cleared | 16 | 66.7 | 2 | 12.5 | 13 | 81.3 | 1 | 33.0 | 1 | 100.0 | 1 | 100.0 | 4 | 40.0 | 1 | 25.0 | 3 | 75.0 |
| Ban on Publication (s.486(3))* | 22 | 91.7 | 2 | 9.1 | 20 | 90.9 | 3 | 100.0 | - | - | 3 | 100.0 | - | - | - | - | - | - |
| Child Testifies Turned Away | 4 | 16.7 | 1 | 25.0 | 3 | 75.0 | - | - | - | - | - | - | 3 | 30.0 | - | - | - | - |
| Microphone | - | - | - | - | - | - | - | - | - | - | - | - | 2 | 20.0 | - | - | - | - |
| Props | - | - | - | - | - | - | - | - | - | - | - | - | 3 | 30.0 | 1 | 33.3 | 3 | 100.0 |
| Expert as Interpreter | - | - | - | - | - | - | - | - | - | - | - | - | 1 | 10.0 | 1 | 100.0 | - | - |
| Expert Testifies re Child's Testimony | 5 | 20.8 | 5 | 100.0 | 2 | 40.0 | - | - | - | - | - | - | 5 | 50.0 | 5 | 100.0 | 3 | 60.0 |

\* These procedural items are part of Bill C-15.

### Table B-10  Experience with Procedural Items for Judges by Location

| Item Requested | CALGARY (n=18) | | | | | | HAMILTON (n=8) | | | | | | SASKATOON (n=22) | | | | | |
|---|---|---|---|---|---|---|---|---|---|---|---|---|---|---|---|---|---|---|
| | Requested n | % | Objecting n | % | Allowed n | % | Requested n | % | Objecting n | % | Allowed n | % | Requested n | % | Objecting n | % | Allowed n | % |
| Videotape (s.715.1)* | 3 | 16.7 | 2 | 66.7 | 3 | 100.0 | - | - | - | - | - | - | 3 | 13.6 | 1 | 33.3 | 1 | 100.0 |
| Screens (s.486(2.1))* | 8 | 44.4 | 2 | 25.0 | 8 | 100.0 | 3 | 38.0 | 1 | 33.0 | 1 | 33.0 | 12 | 54.5 | 3 | 25.0 | 12 | 100.0 |
| Booster Seat | 1 | 5.6 | - | - | 1 | 100.0 | 2 | 25.0 | - | - | 1 | 50.0 | 6 | 27.3 | 1 | 16.7 | 5 | 83.3 |
| Child Brings Toy | - | - | - | - | - | - | - | - | - | - | - | - | 8 | 36.4 | - | - | 8 | 100.0 |
| Child Sits on Knee | 1 | 5.6 | - | - | 1 | 100.0 | - | - | - | - | - | - | 2 | 9.1 | 1 | 50.0 | 2 | 100.0 |
| Adult Accompanied to Stand | 4 | 22.2 | - | - | 3 | 75.0 | 1 | 13.0 | - | - | 1 | 100.0 | 10 | 45.5 | 6 | 60.0 | 10 | 100.0 |
| Support Adult in Court | 14 | 77.8 | 2 | 14.3 | 10 | 71.4 | 3 | 38.0 | 1 | 33.0 | 3 | 100.0 | 17 | 77.3 | 5 | 29.4 | 16 | 94.1 |
| Witnesses Cleared | 13 | 72.2 | 4 | 30.8 | 11 | 84.6 | 5 | 63.0 | 1 | 20.0 | 4 | 80.0 | 19 | 86.4 | 6 | 31.6 | 18 | 94.7 |
| Spectators Cleared | 11 | 61.1 | 4 | 36.4 | 9 | 81.8 | 5 | 63.0 | 1 | 20.0 | 2 | 40.0 | 17 | 77.3 | 7 | 41.2 | 13 | 76.5 |
| Ban on Publication (s.486(3))* | 16 | 88.9 | 1 | 6.3 | 13 | 81.3 | 6 | 75.0 | 1 | 17.0 | 5 | 83.0 | 20 | 90.9 | - | - | 17 | 89.5 |
| Child Testifies Turned Away | 4 | 22.2 | 1 | 25.0 | 4 | 100.0 | 1 | 13.0 | - | - | - | - | 9 | 40.9 | 2 | 22.2 | 9 | 100.0 |
| Closed Circuit Television | - | - | - | - | - | - | - | - | - | - | - | - | 1 | 4.5 | - | - | 1 | 100.0 |
| Microphone | - | - | - | - | - | - | - | - | - | - | - | - | 10 | 45.5 | 1 | 10.0 | 10 | 100.0 |
| Expert as Interpreter | 1 | 5.6 | - | - | 1 | 100.0 | - | - | - | - | - | - | 1 | 4.5 | 1 | 100.0 | 1 | 100.0 |
| Expert Testifies re Child's Testimony | 5 | 27.8 | 3 | 60.0 | 4 | 80.0 | - | - | - | - | - | - | 1 | 4.5 | - | - | 1 | 100.0 |

* These procedural items are part of Bill C-15.

**Figure B-1** <u>**Prediction Model for Witness Behaviour: Anxious/Withdrawn for Calgary Court Proceedings**</u>[1]

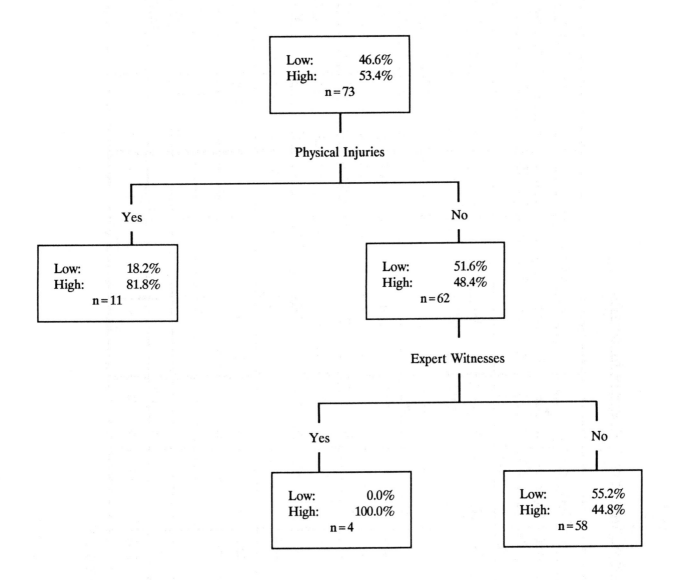

---

[1] Significance Level = .05
Data Sources = 1. Court Observation Schedule
2. Court Observation Rating Scales
3. Police File Review

**Figure B-2** **Prediction Model for Witness Behaviour: Ability to Communicate for Calgary Court Proceedings**[1]

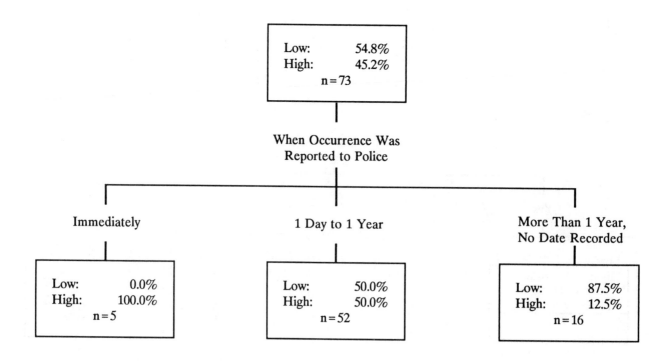

---

[1] Significance Level = .05
Data Sources = 1. Court Observation Schedule
2. Court Observation Rating Scales
3. Police File Review

**Figure B-3**  **Prediction Model for Witness Behaviour: Anxious/Withdrawn for Edmonton Court Proceedings**[1]

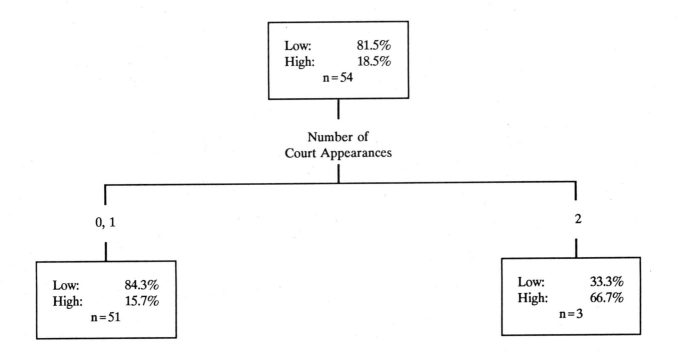

---

[1] Significance Level = .20
Data Sources = 1. Court Observation Schedule
 2. Court Observation Rating Scales
 3. Police File Review

Figure B-4  **Prediction Model for Witness Behaviour: Sad/Cries for Edmonton Court Proceedings**[1]

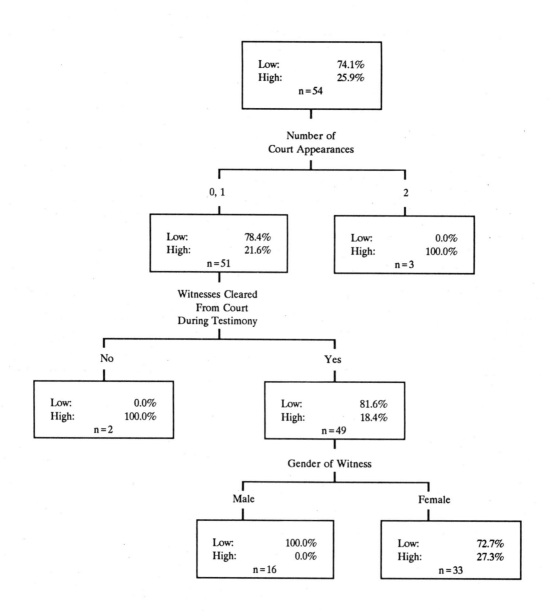

[1] Significance Level = .05
Data Sources = 1. Court Observation Schedule
2. Court Observation Rating Scales
3. Police File Review

**Figure B-5** **Prediction Model for Witness Behaviour: Ability to Communicate for Edmonton Court Proceedings[1]**

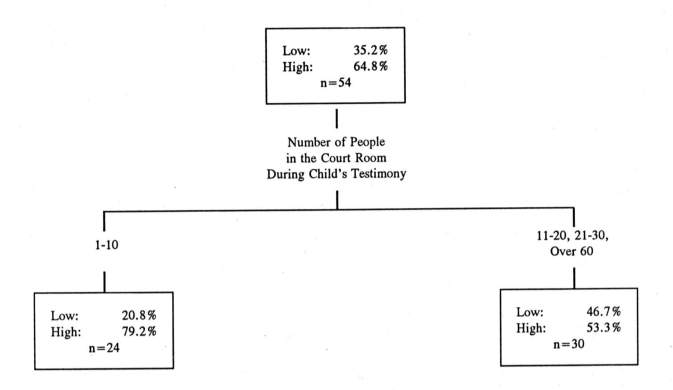

---

[1] Significance Level = .05
Data Sources = 1. Court Observation Schedule
2. Court Observation Rating Scales
3. Police File Review

# APPENDIX C

## REVIEW AND MONITORING OF CHILD SEXUAL ABUSE CASES IN SELECTED SITES IN RURAL ALBERTA: A SUMMARY

by

Donna Phillips, M.S.W., Research Associate
Canadian Research Institute for Law and the Family

Joseph P. Hornick, Ph.D., Executive Director
Canadian Research Institute for Law and the Family

1992

# REVIEW AND MONITORING
# OF CHILD SEXUAL ABUSE CASES
# IN SELECTED SITES IN RURAL ALBERTA: A SUMMARY

## INTRODUCTION

The purpose of this study is to examine how cases of child sexual abuse are processed and treated in the child welfare and justice systems in selected rural communities in Alberta since the implementation of Bill C-15, <u>An Act to Amend the Criminal Code and the Canada Evidence Act</u>. Three rural sites were chosen to provide information which could be compared to the results of a larger study conducted in two large cities, Edmonton and Calgary.

The three rural communities included in the study were: (1) Bassano, (2) Peace River and (3) Gleichen, three very different communities. Bassano is a predominantly Caucasian farming community with a population of around 1200. It is approximately 200 kilometres east of Calgary. Peace River has a population of 6043, and is also predominantly Caucasian with a significant proportion of Native Canadians, Mennonites and Francophones. It is situated 485 kilometres northwest of Edmonton. The Gleichen area is populated by members of the Siksika Nation, which was formerly the Blackfoot Indian Reserve #146. The Reserve covers a geographic area approximately 64 kilometres by 32 kilometres. It is located 90 kilometres east of Calgary. The Reserve has a native population of approximately 3738.

### Method

Due to the small number of cases at the rural sites, a case study approach was used. The three major study components were:

(1)   A review of child welfare files;

(2)   A review of police (RCMP) files; and

(3)   Court observation.

The police file review involved reviewing all cases in which charges were laid or there were court proceedings after January 1, 1988. These were typically closed or concluded cases. Child welfare files for these cases were also reviewed.

From July 31, 1989 to July 31, 1990, all child welfare and police files related to cases that were active during the study period were also reviewed. These cases were typically open, and were discussed on an ongoing basis with the professionals involved. The instruments and procedures for both types of file review were the same as those used in the main study (see Appendix C of <u>Review and Monitoring of Child Sexual Abuse Cases in Selected Sites in Alberta</u>). The methods for observation were also the same as those used in the main study. Many cases were followed closely and were discussed at length with involved professionals.

A total of 43 police files were reviewed: 14 from Bassano, 16 from Peace River and 13 from Gleichen. In Bassano and Gleichen all files open during the study period (January 1, 1988 to July 31, 1990) were reviewed. In Peace River, as the areas covered by the Peace River RCMP and child welfare offices intersected but were not identical, only police files which also fell under the jurisdiction of the Peace River child welfare office were reviewed. A total of 53 child welfare files were reviewed: 13 from Bassano, 13 from Gleichen, and 27 from Peace River.

## CONCLUSIONS

### Case Profile

Rural child sexual abuse cases were found most often to be intrafamilial, occurring in the victim's home. There was a relatively high probability that witnesses, in addition to the victim, would be involved in the case. Victims tended to disclosed to child welfare authorities more often than to family members, and disclosures tended to take place after a longer period of silence than urban disclosures.

Alcohol use was high in rural cases (37 percent), and the use of verbal force was relatively high. In Gleichen the use of physical force was also high (31 percent).

The rate of reporting of child sexual abuse was higher than in Calgary and Edmonton, the proportion of cases cleared by charge was also high, as were the proportion of guilty pleas. In Gleichen, the occurrence of child sexual abuse was 22 percent higher than the highest urban rate. The nature and structure of the native community and culture also made it difficult for victims to disclose. This would suggest that the sexual abuse problem in Gleichen may be more covert than in the other areas. The high number of retractions by victims in the Gleichen area is also indicative of the covert nature of the problem, and of the community pressure on these child victims.

**Bill C-15**

The Bill C-15 provision allowing the use of videotaped disclosures in court has prompted the videotaping of a high proportion of disclosures. However, none of these videotapes were used in court.

Another impact of Bill C-15 appears to be the high level of collaboration between child welfare and criminal justice personnel in the rural areas. Protocols have been established, and a good deal of consultation and joint investigation occurred.

**Specific Native Issues**

The findings of this report suggest the need for natives to administer their own child welfare services. This is especially important because it will help workers understand and deal appropriately with the unique community and cultural dynamics surrounding the sexual abuse of native children. The need for workers to receive the ongoing support of a team approach is also suggested.

**General Rural Issues**

Child welfare workers, police, and crown prosecutors in the rural sites have worked well together on very difficult cases. Such cooperation seems imperative, especially in view of the lack of treatment resources and the geographic distances between some of the key players. The high rate of intrafamilial abuse and the fact that victim families feel isolated and scrutinized by their communities further suggests a definite need for coordinated family interventions.

# BIBLIOGRAPHY

Alberta Family and Social Services. (1987). Protocols: Management of Child Physical and Sexual Abuse Cases. Calgary: Alberta Family and Social Services, Calgary Region.

Alberta Family and Social Services. (1989). Child Welfare Handbook and Program Manual. Edmonton, Alberta Family and Social Services, September.

Achenbach, T. M., & Edelbrock, C. (1983). Manual for the Child Behavior Checklist and Revised Behavior Profile. Burlington, Vermont: Queen City Printers, Inc.

Calgary Police Commission Prostitution Report. (1991). Calgary Police Commission Prostitution Report.

Campbell Research Associates and Social Data Research Ltd. (1992). Review and Monitoring of Child Sexual Abuse Cases in Selected Sites in Hamilton-Wentworth, Ontario. Prepared for: Justice Canada.

Canadian Centre for Justice Statistics. (1990). The Development of Data Quality Assessment Procedures for Uniform Crime Reporting Survey: A Case Study of Calgary/Edmonton. Ottawa: Statistics Canada.

EKOS Research Associates Inc. (1988). Report on the Impacts of the 1983 Sexual Assault Legislation in Hamilton-Wentworth, Department of Justice Canada, Ottawa.

Finkelhor, D. (1986). A Sourcebook on Child Sexual Abuse. Beverly Hills: Sage.

Fischer, D.G., Stevens, G., and Berg, L. (1992). Review and Monitoring of Child Sexual Abuse Cases in Selected Sites in Saskatchewan. Prepared for: Justice Canada by Peat Marwick Stevenson & Kellogg, Management Consultants.

Goodman, G. (1988). The Competency of Child Witnesses. Paper presented at Focus on Child Abuse: New Knowledge, New Directions, Toronto.

Hann, R.J., and Kopelman, S. (1987). Assault: Custodial and Probation Sentences: 1984/85. A Report of the Correctional Sentences Project. Ottawa: Programs and Research Section, Department of Justice Canada

Hornick, J.P., Burrows, B., Perry, D., and Bolitho, F. (1992). <u>Review and Monitoring of Child Sexual Abuse Cases in Selected Sites in Alberta</u>. Prepared for: Justice Canada and Health and Welfare Canada by the Canadian Research Institute for Law and the Family.

Loh, W. D. (1980). The Impact of Common Law and Reform Rape Statutes on Prosecution: An Empirical Study. <u>Washington Law Review, 55</u>, 543-652.

Phillips, D., and Hornick, J.P. (1992). <u>Review and Monitoring of Child Sexual Abuse Cases in Selected Sites in Rural Alberta</u>. Prepared for: Justice Canada and Health and Welfare Canada by the Canadian Research Institute for Law and the Family.

Report of the Committee on Sexual Offences Against Children and Youths. (1984). <u>Sexual Offences Against Children</u> (Vol. I). Ottawa: Minister of Supply and Services Canada.

Roberts, J.V. (1990a). <u>Sexual Assault Legislation in Canada. An Evaluation: Sentencing Patterns in Cases of Sexual Assault, Report No. 3</u>, Department of Justice Canada.

Roberts, J.V. (1990b). <u>Sexual Assault Legislation in Canada. An Evaluation: An Analysis of National Statistics, Report No. 4</u>, Department of Justice Canada.